THE BOOK OF

POOR OULD FELLAS

Declan Lynch lives in Wicklow and writes for the
Sunday Independent. Previous publications include
the acclaimed novel *The Rooms*.

Arthur Mathews is the co-creator of the classic
TV series *Father Ted* and the hit musical *I Keano*.
He lives in Dublin and London.

THE BOOK OF

POOR OULD FELLAS

DECLAN LYNCH
with ARTHUR MATHEWS

HODDER
HEADLINE
IRELAND

First published in 2007 by Hodder Headline Ireland

ISBN 978 0 340 95133 0

Typeset Bulmer by Anú Design, Tara
Cover and book design by Anú Design, Tara
Printed and bound by Clays Ltd, St Ives Plc
Inside illustrations: Arthur Mathews
The publishers would like to thank *The Sunday Independent* and www.freeimages.co.uk
for permission to use inside photos.

Hodder Headline Ireland's policy is to use papers that are natural,
renewable and recyclabe products and made from wood grown in sustainable forests.
The logging and manufacturing processes are expected to conform to the
environmental regulations of the country of origin.

Hodder Headline Ireland
8 Castlecourt Centre
Castleknock
Dublin 15
Ireland

www.hhireland.ie

A division of Hachette Livre, 338 Euston Road, London NW1 3BH, England

Contents

Introduction

Poor ould fellas, as we tend to call them, with that corrosive mixture of pity and indifference, have had their culture virtually wiped out in this country in recent years.

And no one apparently gives a damn.

Their culture is simple and straightforward and demands almost nothing of the rest of us, yet we have destroyed it, and have effectively ruined the lives of all those poor ould fellas who made this country what it is today.

They need just two main things to survive – to be able to have a smoke along with their pint; and to be able to watch some half-decent afternoon TV show on RTÉ, perhaps featuring a song performed by Johnny McEvoy.

And that's about it. That's all these poor ould fellas ask. And it is also reflective of their culture that they ask for these things rarely, in a quiet voice which disturbs no one. Which probably explains why their ancient ways are on the verge of extinction.

Looking at the cover of this book, at that poor ould fella having a drink and a smoke in a bar, it is hard to believe that such an image now belongs to a bygone age. But we've put it there anyway, as a reminder of those better days when a poor ould fella could enjoy some small consolation as he reached the end of life's journey.

But those days are over now. The smoking ban has wrecked whatever social life the poor ould fellas had. And *The Afternoon Show* has done the rest, destroying whatever remains of their days.

Johnny McEvoy never sings on *The Afternoon Show*. Back in the day, it would be quite common for Marty Whelan on *Live At Three* to introduce a song by Johnny McEvoy – "The Boston Burglar", or something – live in the studio, and that was all it took to make a load of poor ould fellas happy.

Now they must look at wall-to-wall women, concerned almost exclusively with women's things. They must look at gay fellows over in Hollywood talking about the latest developments in the plots of soap operas and about various members of the cast of *Desperate Housewives* who have had Botox injections.

They must look at clothes, and cooking, and bullshit from the gossip columns.

Later in the evening, alone with their cigarettes which they aren't allowed to smoke in the pub any more, they watch TV, and still all they want is Johnny McEvoy, once in a blue moon. And all they get is Brian Kennedy, all the time.

But I wouldn't heap all the blame onto *The Afternoon Show* and RTÉ in general.

As a nation, we have failed these men.

There's a story, for example, which comes to us from Waterford, but could come from anywhere in Ireland today. It's the story of a poor ould fella with two wooden legs, who parked his car in an parking for the disabled space, as is his wont.

Astonishingly, he received a €40 ticket because his disabled person's pass had expired six days ago. Yes, for six whole days he had been ineligible to park in this space, perhaps assuming in his naivety that a poor ould fella with two wooden legs might be forgiven this one infringement in the course of an otherwise blameless life.

So what sort of a country is this, where a poor ould fella with not one, but two wooden legs, has to fork out the guts of his miserable old-age pension for such a harmless oversight?

A country called Ireland, my friends, which not only tolerates this kind of abuse of the old, the sick and the handicapped, but actually congratulates itself almost daily on the smoking ban which has destroyed the lives of so many of these poor ould fellas – and not just the ones who smoke.

Our south-east sources are very interesting on this point; the way in which the ban has also destroyed the lives of poor ould fellas who don't smoke at all. Back in the day, a typical morning would see the poor ould fellas shuffling into the pub at around 11 a.m. Who knows how long their day had already been, as the sleep of the poor ould fellas can be fitful at best, and infested by unquiet dreams.

Anyway they would have their pint of stout, at a special price of €2, a "pensioner's pint" as it's called in southern parts. Of course they would have a smoke, a Sweet Afton or two, and together they would peruse the racing pages, making their selections for the afternoon's sport on the pub TV.

Just a few modest bets, a small investment in various doubles, trebles, accumulators and yankees, to give them some vague purpose in life until lunchtime at least.

For the few poor ould fellas who didn't smoke, as well as the vast majority who smoked, this timeless routine would kill the day for them.

So when the smokers were banished, the poor ould fellas who didn't smoke were also screwed – basically, they had no one to talk to any more, because no one talks to poor ould fellas apart from other poor ould fellas, and certainly no one is listening to them.

How do they kill the day now? Is there any way to fathom the emptiness of these men's lives, as they sit at home remembering happier times, like the afternoon when they won forty quid on a yankee, just about enough to pay the fine imposed for parking in the disabled person's space with a technically incorrect pass? Just about enough to forget for a moment that you have two wooden legs?

Obviously these men can't figure out how to get the racing channel, and they couldn't afford it anyway, so they are stuck with *The Afternoon Show*, on which they might learn new life skills, such as how to create a caramelised onion sauce, or how to bake a Ukrainian poppy-seed cake. But these are men whose culinary needs are as simple and as undemanding as any of their other needs.

All they want to eat is some bread, some cheese, and some oxtail soup. And by that I mean normal white sliced bread, a box of Galtee cheese, and oxtail soup that comes out of a packet, and makes one-and-a-half pints, as God intended it.

No celebrity chef can persuade them that cooking is "fun"; they are beyond all that, they can't be fooled by Jamie Oliver. Cooking is not fun, and eating is not fun either. Fun is sitting with your old friends in a friendly bar, supping a pensioner's pint and smoking a cigarette and waiting for the racing to start. For the poor ould fellas, there is no other fun to be had. And anyone who suggests otherwise has not been looking at daytime TV of late.

Would it be too much to ask for someone like Ted Walsh to be given a slot on *The Afternoon Show*, giving tips for the big races at least? After all, the housewives are also partial to a flutter on the big races, so that would make it all right, wouldn't it?

It's not going to happen though, no more than Johnny McEvoy is suddenly going to materialise beside the ladies on the couch, singing "The Boston Burglar". Those days are gone, like the pensioner's pint, the lumps of white bread soaking in the oxtail soup in a metallic bowl, and that long, satisfying smoke as the poor ould fella calms his shattered nerves, collecting his meagre winnings with trembling hands at the pay-out window – no, he can't smoke in the betting office either.

He can do nothing now, but wait…

TELEVISION

Three Channels and Nothing On

When I publicly raised the issue of the poor ould fellas and the way that their last few pleasures have been taken away from them, the response was immediate and overwhelming.

From the reaction to that first piece in the *Sunday Independent*, it would appear that the nation had been well aware that it has failed these men but had been keeping quiet about it.

Now, in letters and emails and phone calls, people could express their feelings of sorrow and anger, and also their feelings of guilt.

Then again, for people with busy lives and three thousand TV channels to choose from, until these matters are explicitly brought to their attention it may be just too hard to relate to the lifestyle problems of poor ould fellas who don't get out much and who are mostly reliant on three channels: RTÉ One and RTÉ Two and possibly TV3 or TG4 – nothing there for them, obviously, though TG4 once ran a series of cowboy pictures which some of them caught by accident.

Certainly there seemed to be a fair few Johnny McEvoy fans out there who had a shock of recognition when we pointed out that these poor ould fellas ask for nothing but the odd Johnny McEvoy song on daytime TV. One reader suggested a more sinister aspect to this sorry state of affairs.

Poor ould fellas, he explained, are of no interest to advertisers. They buy almost nothing. Obviously they don't buy clothes or anything which could be called food.

If they have been drinking Redbreast for the last sixty years, it would take a pretty impressive effort from the advertisers to make them switch to Bacardi Breezer at this stage. They can't be persuaded to take up new things, and they can't be persuaded to give up things either – a government anti-smoking TV campaign won't reach them, because what's the point? They're almost dead anyway.

They don't buy anything for themselves, nor do they buy anything for anyone else. They back horses, but they wouldn't be Paddy Power's most valued customers, with their sad few shillings and their reluctance to flash those credit cards, which they don't have anyway, to open an Internet account. No, these men don't conduct much business online.

So with their almost total lack of spending power, they are simply ignored by the makers of daytime TV – and night-time TV, if it comes to that, which it rarely does, as the poor ould fellas are slipping into a sort of a coma by then.

Their exclusion from TV's rich banquet would perhaps be understandable if RTÉ was running a purely commercial operation, but of course it is supposed to be catering for minority tastes as well, as part of its public-service remit. And there is no more oppressed minority than these poor ould fellas, who face discrimination, not just on grounds of age and infirmity, nor on account of their ancient culture, but also because they have no money – or at least they have no interest in shopping.

So poor ould fellas are ignored by the makers of daytime TV because they are poor, because they are ould and because they are fellas.

They try not to be bitter about it, but it's awfully hard for them. They are not against women, as such, presenting these programmes. They used to like the homely Mary Kennedy, for example, when she hosted *Live at Three* alongside Marty Whelan. And they still like her when she hosts *Nationwide* alongside Michael Ryan, a programme which occasionally does an item about a trout-fishing competition or a ploughing festival, something that the poor ould fellas can relate to, a bit of diversion after the six o'clock news.

Sadly, some bullshit about cooking or pottery or candles or aromatherapy is never too far away, but it's not all bad.

Nor do they have any objection to the same Mary Kennedy hosting *Up for the Match* alongside Des Cahill.

Up for the Match, therefore, is a programme which persuades the poor ould fellas to stay up after the news on the eve of the hurling and football finals – though they are always disappointed by it and they are reconciled to the fact that there'll be no Johnny McEvoy here either.

Two nights a year, then, there's some all-round entertainment for the poor ould fellas. Something that they think will be good but usually turns out to be bad.

Time was when *The Riordans* assured them of at least one programme a week which they could enjoy, with great ould characters like Batty Brennan, himself a poor ould fella of iconic stature.

But gradually even rural soap operas started going to the bad, until the nadir was reached one day on *Emmerdale Farm* when a farmer – admittedly an English farmer, but a farmer nonetheless – was seen working in a room in his farmhouse which can only be described as an office. And in that office, he was doing his accounts. Yes, his accounts.

The poor ould fellas had seen enough.

It will be claimed by smart-arse TV executives that there's still something for the poor ould fellas every night of the week if you count the Weather. And it is true that the poor ould fellas are devoted to the Weather – to such an extent that there was a serious effort on the part of RTÉ to change it forever. To destroy it, essentially.

For the poor ould fellas, the Angelus, the News and the Weather, in that order, were always a holy thing, a sort of Blessed Trinity which could not be changed in any way without irreparable damage being done to their whole way of life.

So naturally RTÉ set about implementing that change. No one asked for it, but they were going to get it anyway, this new improved Weather with a vital difference – it would be presented by people who weren't qualified to talk about the weather.

They were not meteorologists, they were just "presenters"

who could perform a script written by people who actually knew what they were talking about.

The poor ould fellas were aghast. They had suffered in silence without all the grand old shows of yesteryear like *The Virginian* or *Colombo* or *Ironside*, and now they would suffer even more in silence as this profoundly important matter was handed over to a bunch of amateurs to give them a bit of experience in front of the cameras before they went on to the big RTÉ stuff – perhaps even a career presenting programmes in the afternoon for women.

The poor ould fellas knew that this was horribly, horribly wrong, but of course they said nothing. They remembered when the Weather was presented by some of the ugliest men on earth and it made no difference. Because those men knew what they were talking about.

And amazingly, in the end, RTÉ backed down. They decided not to destroy the Weather after all, not because of complaints from the poor ould fellas, but because of complaints from other people, people who matter.

So the poor ould fellas still have the Weather, presented by people who actually understand what they're saying, as distinct from people who are just making noise. But the Angelus is going downhill, the holy picture of yore replaced by moving pictures of folks who don't necessarily believe in organised religion but who like to pause for a moment's reflection now and again as part of a holistic approach.

It must have been hard for RTÉ to find a way of destroying the Angelus, which was just a few bongs and a holy picture after all, but they managed it somehow.

Nor do the weekends offer much TV solace to the poor ould fellas. There was a series on Sunday nights called *Townlands* which was vaguely like *Nationwide* without Mary Kennedy or anyone alongside her, a series which perhaps had something for the poor ould fellas, but not a lot.

At a stretch, they would have enjoyed one programme in the series, which was about a choir in County Clare. They, or perhaps their wives, who will outlive them for all the wrong reasons, would have called this "a nice programme". Usually it is the wives who put their feelings about TV shows into words. They are the vocal ones, which is probably why their needs are so extensively catered for on *The Afternoon Show* and most other shows that aren't *The Sunday Game*.

The poor ould fellas would think that this *Townlands* was "a nice programme", with its pictures of the Burren and the lovely singing of the choir made up of ordinary Clare people singing Mozart. They would also think it was well timed on a Sunday evening, when they can take a bit of Mozart as they drift off to sleep. But they wouldn't say it.

They would say nothing, because they realised a long time ago that no one is listening to them.

So we must be their voice.

Townlands followed the massively popular *You're a Star*, which is not exactly "a nice programme", as judge Linda Martin would annoy them in some intangible way. They would think that judge Brendan O'Connor has a bit of jizz in him, and they would not understand the hostility between judge Martin and judge O'Connor, though they would broadly welcome it. Judge Thomas Black from the music industry would mean nothing to them.

As for picking the winner, obviously they wouldn't be texting their votes or waiting up till after the nine o'clock news in a state of mounting excitement to hear the verdict.

But if they had a vote, they would probably try to vote for Johnny McEvoy.

So the weekend brings little respite. And the final insult for these men comes on Saturday night, when they see that someone like Tara Palmer-Tomkinson is on *Tubridy Tonight* or any of the other talk shows that hire Tara to do whatever the hell she does.

She can talk, perhaps, but why? That is the question. Why is this woman sitting there talking?

There is actually no excuse for any talk show to be anything but brilliant every week, since they have the top people in every walk of life queuing up for a bit of airtime to promote things which are actually good, but somehow, incredibly, they keep booking Tara Palmer-Tomkinson and her ilk.

It is cold comfort for the poor ould fellas that they're missing nothing, sitting there in a coma, with Tara talking.

Cold comfort indeed.

The Poor Ould Fella's
IDEAL
TV Schedule

1.00 The News
The latest headlines.

2.00 Colombo
A case of mistaken identity leads to trouble for the raincoat-wearing detective.

3.00 Racing from the Curragh
Ted Walsh presents.

5.00 Ironside
A case of mysterious food poisoning leads to trouble for the wheelchair-bound detective.

6.00 The Angelus

6.01 The News
The latest headlines.

7.00 All-Ireland Gold
A nostalgic look through the archives. This week's programme features Down v Offaly from 1961.

7.30 Johnny McEvoy in Concert
The popular singer recorded at the Cork Opera House in 1977.

8.00 Glenroe
A repeat of the popular rural drama.

9.00 The News
The latest headlines.

9.25 The Late Late Show
Pat Kenny is replaced by Gay Byrne for this special nostalgic edition.

11.15 Late News
The latest headlines.

11.20 Closedown

The Poor Ould Fella's
NIGHTMARE
TV Schedule

1.00 The Anna Nolan Show
A special four-hour-long edition presented by the lesbian *Big Brother* contestant.

5.00 The Best of Graham Norton
Highlights from the outrageous gay comedian's last series.

6.00 South Park

7.00 Video Exclusive
An exclusive preview of Marilyn Manson's new video, "Fuck You".

7.10 Gordon Ramsay Goes Mad in a Kitchen
Foul language as top celebrity chef Gordon Ramsay goes mad in a kitchen.

8.00 Trinny and Susannah
The fashion gurus dress a lesbian factory worker from Newcastle.

9.00 Jamie's School Dinners
More cookery.

10.00 Inside Porn Valley
California's sex industry explored.

11.00 Footballers' Wives
A double episode of the popular series.

12.00 Designer Vaginas
A repeat of this controversial show first aired in 2003.

1–5am All The Hits
Hip-hop and dance videos.

I'm looking forward to the second part of Colombo. I don't think the black fella did it...

fuck-you-poor-ould-fellas@RTÉ.ie

Just as the poor ould fellas had given up all hope and resigned themselves to the eternal darkness that is *The Afternoon Show*, there was an announcement from RTÉ which seemed, if anything, to be rubbing their noses in it.

It was proposed that Gráinne Seoige would be presenting an afternoon chat-show on RTÉ One, which was not exactly good news for our old friends, the poor ould fellas. At least they are old friends of ours, and we strive to represent their interests while everyone else seems to take inordinate pleasure in making their already miserable lives even more unbearable.

Apparently RTÉ bosses felt that *The Afternoon Show* wasn't quite enough: there was a need for another show in the afternoon presented by a woman with whom the poor ould fellas would have absolutely no affinity.

So just as the *The Afternoon Show* would be winding down for the day, with a few tips about cookery for gay couples or a feature on New World wines or some bollocks about celebrities doing aerobics, the details of which can be found on the website, the poor ould fellas would have to face in to Gráinne Seoige and another hour of total alienation.

Even still, they had perhaps not entirely given up hope

in relation to Seoige. Despite her celebrity status, she has something of that homely quality possessed by Mary Kennedy and the newsreader Eileen Dunne, and of course Seoige also used to read the news, which will always stand to her.

But they are troubled by her Irish name, as indeed they are troubled by the Irish name of Sharon Ní Bheoláin, another woman who reads the news in a homely fashion but who is also suspected by the ould fellas of harbouring showbiz ambitions. They figure that broadcasting is now like the civil service used to be, that if you want to get ahead in this country, you need that Irish bullshit.

So the poor ould fellas haven't totally abandoned Seoige and Ní Bheoláin as they have abandoned so many other women, but the question remains in their poor ould heads: are these ladies entirely to be trusted, the way that, say, Thelma Mansfield could be trusted in days of yore?

Are they to be trusted as Bibi Baskin came to be trusted?

Bibi was The Special One. She went in for the glitz and the glamour, like the rest of them, but she somehow managed to do this while presenting programmes that poor ould fellas could watch, programmes with country people in them, singing and telling stories about long ago.

She even went in for that that Irish-speaking bullshit without giving you a pain in the head.

As a result, she was forever opening festivals in country towns, the big noise from RTÉ who could speak to the folks in rural Ireland in their own tongue. And betimes the poor ould fellas could be seen on the edge of the crowd when Bibi came to town, staring at The Special One as she cut the ribbon on a new supermarket.

Satisfied by what they had seen, they would park the ould bike outside a friendly bar and drink bottles of porter for the rest of the day, thinking fond thoughts of Bibi Baskin, who had arrived in the big flash car but who was still very down to earth.

Naturally they wouldn't say this to anyone, because they are not the sort of men who debate the merits of TV personalities – such talk is the mark of the dreamer, the fellow who isn't all there, the eejit.

But if they heard some eejit saying that Bibi was "very down to earth", they wouldn't object. And when some eejit on the radio was asked about his funeral arrangements and he said that he'd like to be "buried up to his balls in Bibi Baskin", they didn't object to that either.

No, they felt that had a ring to it.

They had come to regard Bibi Baskin with a grudging respect, earned over a long period of time presenting shows aimed at the forgotten tribes of rural Ireland.

And what happened next? Was Bibi given the job of presenting *The Late Late Show*?

Did she become Ireland's highest-paid broadcaster by dint of her unique appeal to viewers across the demographic spectrum, an appeal so broad it even encompassed the poor ould fellas?

Well no, that's not what happened next. Not exactly.

What happened next was that Bibi Baskin gave up broadcasting altogether, withdrew from public life and went to India, where she opened an hotel.

Which surprised a lot of people at the time, but which came as no surprise whatsoever to the poor ould fellas who have seen every other good thing disappear, so why should Bibi be any different?

It is understandable then that when the poor ould fellas are confronted with Gráinne Seoige they are perhaps slow to give her an unqualified vote of confidence. Seoige may know things about the world beyond glitzy weddings and chick-flicks, and if she was let, she could probably hold forth with some authority on subjects which are of interest to poor ould fellas, such as horse-racing and the music of Johnny McEvoy.

But would she ever be let?

When Seoige first joined RTÉ, the smart money said that she wouldn't be let near any of that stuff which the poor ould fellas like and which used to be down for consideration, at least, in the realm of public-service broadcasting. In fact, there was a time, long ago, when poor ould fellas used to be actually allowed to sit in a studio audience, enjoying the afternoon fare on a show called *Going Strong*.

Incredible as it now seems, viewers were shown pictures of poor ould fellas sitting there just like real people, even speaking from time to time. They weren't allowed to smoke in the studio, but that was about the only place they weren't allowed to smoke, due to the more humane attitude which prevailed at that time.

A poor ould fella might even open his mouth and sing, as he sat there in the studio, trying to enjoy his last few days above ground, just trying to stay alive at least until the six o'clock news.

Now they are banished, out of sight, out of mind.

No doubt RTÉ would welcome their emails on this and any other subject. So if you're a poor ould fella looking for something that might kill the day for you, and if you know what an email is, which you almost certainly don't, the address is fuck-you-poor-ould-fellas@rte.ie.

Or walk to your neighbours' house four miles away and ask them if you can use their laptop to send an email. Yes, that would definitely kill the day for you.

And of course, check out the Fuck-you-poor-ould-fellas website.

Things that make absolutely no difference to the life of a Poor Ould Fella:

Global warming
Opening of the port tunnel
Low interest charges on credit cards
Mortgage relief
Chick-lit
The need for another runway at Dublin Airport
Posh and Becks
J-Lo
China
eBay
The God Delusion
Science

The Afternoon Show – "Tackling Bullying in Cyberspace"

For the poor ould fellas, the start of a new season of *The Afternoon Show* merely confirmed all of their darkest forebodings. Not only was it not going away any time soon, on the contrary, RTÉ was obviously persevering with it until it was totally free of anything relevant to the poor ould fellas.

So when it all started up again, you'd see odd things, like the presenters looking into the wrong camera, reminding the poor ould fellas of the RTÉ of yesteryear. But otherwise there was nothing in it for them.

There was a chef, for example, making what he called a "roo". Or maybe a "roux". Or something similarly French and beyond the ken of the poor ould fellas, who have come such a long way down life's highway to end up sitting alone on a busted couch watching some fellow dishing up something that looked like "peasant food", as it's called, and making a roo. Or maybe a rue. Something that isn't oxtail soup, at any rate, or cheese sandwiches, the only sort of "peasant food" that the poor ould fellas can relate to, the sort of "peasant food" that is actually eaten by peasants, as distinct from flamboyant characters who run their own PR companies.

The sort of characters, perhaps, who can be found in RTÉ, looking at a fellow making a roo and thinking that the poor ould fellas are out there now, loving this, and maybe taking notes, so that they can surprise all their friends with this new recipe the next time they're entertaining.

Entertaining? We don't think so. We really don't think so.

We think the poor ould fellas have done all the entertaining they're ever going to be doing. And likewise, they have received all the entertaining they're ever going to get in this TV world which has apparently discarded singers of the calibre of Johnny McEvoy and replaced them with fellows cooking.

And these fellows have the women watching them cooking, and tasting the bit of grub afterwards, and saying it's the most beauuuuutiful thing they ever ate in all their lives, and how did they get it to taste so beauuuuutiful, aren't they the great fellows altogether?

Sheana Keane, it was, watching the fellow cooking on the first programme. This would be the same Sheana Keane who returned to *The Afternoon Show*, having left it after the first series. So now she was back, replacing Anna Nolan.

To the poor ould fellas it looked like they were shuffling

the deck here – like they thought that Sheana was wrong, so she left, but then they thought she was all right after all, it was Anna Nolan who was wrong. And maybe for the next series they'll decide that Nolan was all right after all, it's the other one, Blathnaid Ní Chofaigh, who is wrong.

To the poor ould fellas, it has been perfectly clear right from the start – THEY'RE ALL FUCKING WRONG.

This programme, in every respect, is all wrong, without so much as one half-decent man at the helm, without even Marty Whelan, and without any singing of any description by any of our leading artistes.

It is not right.

It is wrong.

This whole world is all wrong if you're unfortunate enough to be a poor ould fella. Which at least half of you will be, one of these days, whether you like it or not.

Then, and only then, will you truly know the pain of watching the two ladies (and then there were two) signing off with the immortal words, "tomorrow we'll be tackling the issue of cyber-bullying".

Will ye, now? Will ye be doing the nation that vital service?

Cyber-bullying, whatever that is, seems to be an "issue" that requires "tackling". The abandonment of an entire race of men of a certain age and a certain sensibility doesn't seem to bother anyone in any position of influence. Apparently that's not an issue at all.

The poor ould fellas have seen terrible things in their lives – they have seen war and hunger and grief and wretchedness of every description – and now in their last days, they can only watch as the finest minds of daytime TV devote their energies to this grave problem which they have identified, this thing they call cyber-bullying.

Bullying the poor ould fellas out of their few modest pleasures on this earth, forcing them out of the pubs to allow a tribe of middle-class pen-pushers to have their "carvery lunch" in a smoke-free environment, all this is evidently a mere trifle next to the over-riding public menace posed by cyber-bullying.

Tonight, another batch of poor ould fellas will shuffle off, dying because they just can't stand living any more, and what will RTÉ producers be thinking about in their plush offices? They'll be thinking about cyber-bullying. They'll be banging their fists on the table and saying that something must be done about all this cyber-bullying, as the coffin of another poor ould fella is lowered into a pauper's grave and the padre mutters a few words of solace to a poor ould dog called Mick, who on this occasion appears to be the chief mourner.

The only one.

Celebrity Chefs they like

Monica Carr
Keith Floyd

Celebrity Chefs they don't like

Conrad Gallagher
Paul Rankin
Jeanne Rankin
Gordon Ramsay
Neven Maguire
Gary Rhodes
Jamie Oliver
Nigella Lawson
Richard Corrigan
Ainsley Harriot
Hugh Fearnley-Whittingstall
Rick Stein
Antony Worrall Thompson
Anton Mosimann
The Roux Brothers

Darina Allen
Rachel Allen
Tim Allen

she kept it very simple...

The Johnny McEvoy-Shaped Hole

Perhaps television might learn something from another branch of showbusiness where they have not entirely forgotten the poor ould fellas. I refer to the Legends of Irish Folk concerts at the Cork Opera House and the Gaiety Theatre, which went some way towards filling that Johnny McEvoy-shaped hole.

And the Legends of Irish Folk happened at a particularly difficult time for the poor ould fellas, that time of year when RTÉ's autumn schedule appears, promising another load of shows which exclude the poor ould fellas.

Yet, in a deeply poignant way, the autumn schedules are still important to the poor ould fellas, because it needs to be emphasised they are still actually relying on RTÉ to maintain some quality of life – a truly frightening situation, one of those classic nightmarish visions which haunt the elderly, like ending up in the County Home or not having enough money to pay for a Christian burial.

In that context, you can understand that the poor ould fellas don't exactly explode with mirth when they see those traditional pictures of Ryan Tubridy and Pat Kenny clowning around on the RTÉ lawn at the launch of the new season.

For them this is not a laughing matter. Nor is their mood lightened by the announcement of the return of *The Afternoon*

Show, as certainly at no point in the proceedings will any presenter on that show turn to the camera and introduce a song by Johnny McEvoy. Which is all that poor ould fellas ask from life, at this late stage, and which would be happening on any well-run TV station, given the popularity of the aforementioned Legends of Irish Folk concerts, which featured, among others, a certain Mr J. McEvoy.

Of course, the poor ould fellas didn't actually attend the concerts in the Cork Opera House and the Gaiety, because when they see the ads for tickets priced €27.50 with a €2.50 booking fee, they assume that this is not for them. As the song says, they've lived a life that's full, without ever coming close to paying thirty quid for a night in a theatre – including a "booking fee", which they assume is only available on the Internet, or something, and is thus beyond their ken.

Throw in another fifty quid for a taxi from their remote cottage – their shack, to tell the truth – for men who have vivid memories of paying fifty quid for their first car, which kept going for five hundred thousand miles, and you can partly understand why these days the poor ould fellas get most of their entertainment on the box. If they get it at all.

And would Mick the dog still be around when they got back, or would he be lying there dead after being blown away with a sawn-off shotgun wielded by a couple of lads just out of Mountjoy who are always robbing poor ould fellas in isolated areas, because they think for some strange reason that poor ould fellas might have something worth robbing. Clearly these criminal masterminds figure that if a man is living alone in conditions of abject squalor, it stands to reason that he must be extremely wealthy and that his lonesome hovel is actually filled with vast quantities of cash and jewellery. It's obvious, isn't it?

Still, though the poor ould fellas didn't make it to Cork or Dublin to see these Legends of Irish Folk, also dubbed "A Parcel of Rogues", it did their hearts good just to look at the ads and to think fond thoughts of a concert featuring artistes such as Ronnie Drew and Finbar Furey and Paddy Reilly and Johnny McEvoy. Especially Ronnie Drew. And most especially Johnny McEvoy.

The fact that Johnny's still out there, playing concerts, gives them at least some hope that someone in RTÉ might take notice of this and maybe ask him to appear on TV again, preferably during the day when the poor ould fellas are sitting up, at least semi-conscious. Probably the last time they saw Johnny McEvoy on RTÉ was about fifteen years ago in a series about manic depression, which was very good but which RTÉ probably won't show again, because they'd prefer to show something bad, about women.

Then there's the *Legends of Irish Folk* CD, which a lot of poor ould fellas are expecting to be given for Christmas by relations who are well aware that most poor ould fellas don't have a CD player, as they have never in their lives sat listening to a CD, or to a vinyl record for that matter.

They were too busy digging ditches in England, and sending all the money back home to people who don't talk to them any more, to be sitting around listening to albums, rapping about the latest sounds.

But if they can't listen to the CD, they might like looking at the cover anyway, and at the print that is far too small for them to read, on the long dark nights after Samhain.

It's the thought that counts.

Celebrities they like

Bill Cullen
Hector
Eddie Hobbs
Gay Byrne
Eileen Dunne
Derek Davis
Tracey Piggott
Michael Flatley
Bibi Baskin
Thelma Mansfield
Amanda Brunker

Celebrities they don't like

Bob Geldof   Graham Norton
Bono   Celia Larkin
Derek Mooney   Brian Dowling
Louis Walsh   Ray Shah
Kerry Katona   Anna Nolan

CHURCH
AND STATE

The Mistakes of Vatican II

What is the position of the Church in the lives of the poor ould fellas? Certainly they always saw the Church as having a role to play in matters of baptism and burial, the occasional sacraments of penance and communion, and journeys into town to get the Sunday paper and maybe have a few bottles of porter after Mass to kill the day.

They never thought too deeply about it; they were never fanatical but they could be seen kneeling like everyone else, usually at the back of the Church. Usually on one knee, in fact, under which they would place their cap, perhaps to protect the fabric of their trousers or just for ceremonial reasons peculiar to their tribe.

It was all part of what they were, not because they had any great enthusiasm for it, but because they had even less enthusiasm for changing these rigid patterns of behaviour which had apparently served the people well for two thousand years or thereabouts – just about long enough, anyway, for the poor ould fellas to figure that whatever the Church was doing, it was working to some small degree.

And naturally, you wouldn't want to change something like that, would you? If it had taken you centuries to get to where you were, with a stranglehold on Irish society and no

Priests they like

Monsignor Horan of Knock
Bishop Eamonn Casey
Spencer Tracy
Bing Crosby

Priests they don't like

Young priests

He had a great belief in prayer...

end in sight, it wouldn't even cross your mind to start changing things, would it?

Obviously not, if you were a poor ould fella. Yet in the 1960s in the wake of Vatican II, the Catholic Church did exactly that. It changed.

And since then, some of the finest theological minds have spent decades coming to the painful conclusion which was clear to the poor ould fellas from day one – it was all a terrible mistake.

Some of the wise men haven't even accepted this yet, but to the poor ould fellas it is pretty obvious that change was the Church's great enemy, as it is the great enemy of most intelligent life on this planet.

They changed the language of the Mass from Latin to

English to make it more accessible to the people. But the poor ould fellas never wanted it to be accessible in the first place. They wanted to go to a church on a Sunday and get Mass and get the paper and get a few bottles of stout and get home on the bike in one piece, or get a lift home from a neighbour with the bike thrown into the back of the car if they were lucky.

In their entire lives it never crossed their minds for a moment that they might be gaining something if the Mass was made more accessible.

They didn't, in fact, give a monkey about the Mass, as such, as long as they got it. They might have wanted it to be shorter, but they knew that would never happen without radical change, which is the worst type of all. And in the process of that change there was always the risk that it would all go horribly wrong and the Mass would actually end up longer. So they never entertained such thoughts.

Nor did they harbour any great desire for the Church music to change, so that a choir accompanied by a big organ wouldn't be enough any more, you'd also need a Folk Mass with young people playing guitars and flutes and singing pop songs about Jesus.

In their wildest imaginings, it had never entered the heads of the poor ould fellas that such a thing was needed. At no time in their lives had they ever sat in a bar with other poor ould fellas and engaged in a fiery debate about the need for guitars and flutes to be played in church by young people. If they thought about it at all, they figured that the Church might struggle on for another few hundred years with what they had already, all that stuff by Mozart or Beethoven or whoever made up the hymns which had been sung without any complaints from the poor ould fellas every day of the week, every week of the year, every year since records began.

But there were men in Rome who had other thoughts. Wise men, highly educated men, who read the situation differently.

They felt, for example, that the priest shouldn't be spending so much time on the altar with his back turned to the people. Instead of talking to God in Latin, he should turn around and talk to the people in their own language. And perhaps some of the people agreed with this, but for that section of the people we call the poor ould fellas, this was all complete and utter bullshit.

In fact, they liked it better when the priest was facing the other way, getting on with it, keeping himself to himself, babbling away in a foreign tongue. At least there was no danger then that he was going to march down from the altar with a big friendly smile and take them by the hand and offer them the dreaded sign of peace.

The poor ould fellas hate that. The only thing they hate more than being offered the sign of peace at Mass is being hugged. And they live in fear of the day that that will happen to them too, that some eejit will turn to them there in the church and offer them the sign of peace by hugging them – maybe the priest himself, sweeping down from the altar, looking to shake things up a bit because he's tired of the old routine.

In fact, of all the innovations brought in since Vatican II, surveys show that there is one above all the others which has made the poor ould fellas stop going to Mass altogether. It is that one chilling line, "Let us offer each other the sign of peace."

A poor ould fella will never voluntarily offer the sign of peace. He will stand there shivering, keeping himself to himself, hoping against hope that others will sense his discomfort and just leave him alone while they get on with their embarrassing handshakes and their fake smiles.

Sometimes he gets away with it. But most of the time he is forced to give the paw, to engage in that excruciating moment of false intimacy with a total stranger. And all this because the fine fellows at Vatican II thought that the old Mass hadn't enough jizz in it.

Things got livelier for them, to be sure, when the papers started showing pictures of paedophile priests emerging from Court Number One charged with 473 counts of child sex abuse. It was all a bit beyond the ken of the poor ould fellas, but they couldn't help thinking that it

would never have come to this if priests had kept talking to God in Latin with their backs turned to the crowd instead of trying to be all-round entertainers.

And as for all the paedophile priests who were at it before 1960 ... sometimes, late in the evening, the poor ould fellas start thinking back through their lives and wondering if certain things that happened to them might be classed as part of this paedophile-priest thing. But it was all so common at the time, and so accepted, even encouraged by the people, in all fairness the poor ould fellas wouldn't feel right about getting their €300,000 compensation like everyone else.

Whatever happened back then, with the priest flailing away, lost to the world in some frenzy of perversion, the poor ould fellas feel it probably hasn't done them much harm. And if it has, they might be required to talk to a solicitor and then to some psychiatrist or therapist, and frankly, that probably wouldn't be worth €300,000 at the end of the day. Especially when you can't think of anything worth buying.

The poor ould fellas hate all that stuff, all that talking. Because that's all that the fellows in the white coats are able to do – talk.

They hate it nearly as much as the sign of peace, but not quite as much, because there are ways of avoiding the head-shrinkers, but there's almost no way of avoiding the sign of peace except to give up your religion.

Which a lot of people have done, for a lot of reasons, since the aforementioned Vatican II.

And in order to lure them back, the Church lays on weddings and funerals with a Las Vegas flavour, with corny songs by Chris de Burgh. Anything, in fact, which repels the poor ould fellas is becoming an intrinsic part of the show, a trend which reached its apogee when Midnight Mass in certain areas was made an all-ticket affair.

Yes, in some parts, in order to get into Midnight Mass, conveniently starting at ten o'clock, you now have to book in advance, because the middle classes were complaining about drunks arriving late to "get Mass" and to widdle in the holy water font. And in excluding these undesirables from the house of God, as a bonus they also exclude the poor ould fellas, who reject the concept of Midnight Mass as an all-ticket affair with every fibre of their being.

So when they're listening to the wireless and they hear

people in any walk of life talking about change and the need for it, the poor ould fellas start arguing with the wireless. They point out that before it changed the Catholic Church was the most powerful institution in Ireland and one of the most powerful in the history of the world. And its priests were regarded as gods.

After the change, when everything had settled down, the condition of the Church in Ireland could best be summed up by the fact that virtually the only priests left in Ireland were elderly men in nursing homes* – a poignant image there for the poor ould fellas. And fifty years of folly was complete when it was learned that they were looking for priests from Africa. They were looking for black men to come to Ireland to spread the faith. Because no Irishman who was half normal would do it.

"Change is good" is the constant message on the wireless from the in-crowd.

But for the Catholic Church, the poor ould fellas muse, change was not good.

Change was bad.

Change was very bad indeed.

Note: Elderly priests are not regarded as poor ould fellas for the purposes of this investigation. Though they may be poor, and they may be ould, and they may be fellas, they have wielded considerable power in their time and set themselves apart from their fellow men with their Catholic garb. They are similar in certain respects but ultimately a different species.

The General Election of 2007 - Part I

Though they would say anything to get elected, and spend vast sums on a bullshit campaign, and pump the hand of every voter in every constituency, the Fianna Fáil party had already been quietly abandoned by thousands of voters who could be found all over the country – I refer, of course, to the poor ould fellas.

With the certainty that there would be a general election in 2007, in every constituency in Ireland the desperately unhappy lives of these men were hanging by a thread, with just one thing to keep them going for another day, one vision that sustained them, one good thought – that some day this general election would be called and they would be able to get themselves to a polling station somehow and vote against this government, which had totally destroyed their lives.

All over Ireland, there were poor ould fellas with about fourteen different forms of terminal illness, who were determined to keep breathing somehow until they exercised their franchise for what would undoubtedly be the last time. They were simply refusing to die until they did this one good thing.

Doctors were baffled, as they solemnly informed a poor ould fella that he had about a week to live and the poor ould fella shuffled away, apparently doomed. And yet a week later he had not died but was looking for more pills. And a month would go by and still he would cling to life. Six months later and, incredibly, the poor ould fella is still among the ranks of the undead, confounding the medics, who cannot understand what is sparking this awesome determination to defy the Reaper.

Many times they have seen the triumph of the human spirit in the face of terrible odds, but they have never seen anything like the utter refusal of the poor ould fellas to die until they had voted against the government in the 2007 general election.

Perhaps deep down the Fianna Fáil wizards were aware of this phenomenon, which is why they were reluctant to go to

Taoisigh they like

Sean Lemass

He wasn't the worst of them...

the country until the last possible moment, refusing to believe that so many poor ould fellas could stay alive for so long.

But they stayed alive. The poor ould fellas would have their revenge on the men who introduced the smoking ban.

They would do their duty, dragging themselves down to the polling station with one last superhuman effort, and then they would go home, the only place they can have a smoke in peace, and they would watch the election special.

For once, they wouldn't have to search in vain for something that might kill the day for them. For once, as the number-crunchers discovered how the poor ould fellas had voted, Ireland would be aware of their presence.

Alone, all alone in their hovels, the poor ould fellas would watch the election special all day, and all of the night, sustained by a large plate of Galtee cheese sandwiches and a packet of oxtail soup, which makes one-and-a-half pints.

Not only would they relish the sight of Fianna Fáilers and PDs falling, they also would take an almost childlike pleasure in the fact that, for one day at least, they would be spared *The Afternoon Show*.

In a best-case scenario, as the Taoiseach conceded the election, they would die happy.

And there was nothing the Taoiseach could do about it either. Because there was just one thing his government forgot to take away from the poor ould fellas – the vote.

Certainly it was futile for Fianna Fáil to try to appeal to the poor ould fellas by pointing to its "achievements" in office. Its achievements include the smoking ban, of course, a form

of ethnic cleansing which most callously drove the poor ould
fellas away from their natural habitats forever.

And its achievements include bypasses and ring roads,
which further aggravated the condition of the poor ould fellas
who can still somehow afford to drive a car. Not a Range
Rover, mind, with bull bars, for journeys to the multiplex
where they might watch a rom com starring Jennifer Aniston
while they munch a portion of nachos with a hot cheese and
chilli dip. Just an ould car to take them as far as town.

From Roscommon, word reaches us that a poor ould fella
who took the same route into town for fifty years, who endured
much in what was not an easy life, had finally been defeated
by various roundabouts which have effectively barred him
from ever entering his home town again under his own steam.

Increasingly, one hears disturbing tales of poor ould
fellas deeply traumatised by their experiences on bypasses,
ring roads and roundabouts. Gripped by a rush of fear that

their short journey into Roscommon town will bring them ultimately to Dublin city centre, swept along by forces beyond their ken, they panic.

So they drive around the roundabout, round and round, frozen with fear, terrified of making the wrong move and causing traffic chaos, at which point the horns will start blaring and they will be subjected to a tirade of abuse by various arseholes in jeeps.

But eventually they'd get off that roundabout too, and they'd go home, and sit down, and with trembling hands they'd light a cigarette. And wait …

Politicians they like

Charlie McCreevy
Mussolini
Brendan McGahon (spirited campaign
against betting tax)

Politicians they don't like

Micheál Martin (architect of smoking ban)
And "all the others who stood idly by"

The General Election of 2007 – Part II

For one strange week, in the autumn of 2006, the hearts of the poor ould fellas were beating just a little bit faster. As the Taoiseach got himself all tangled up in matters arising from the Tribunal, trying to explain the "dig-out" he got from friends and associates, for a few brief moments the poor ould fellas allowed themselves to hope.

Deep down they felt that this hope would eventually be dashed, as all other hope has been dashed. But when there's even a hint, a vague rumour of a general election, they have to enjoy it as best they can, if only because such fleeting moments of pleasure might raise their spirits for the struggle ahead – the struggle to stay alive somehow until May 2007, when they would drag themselves down to the polling station to give Bertie and his government what's coming to them.

So there they were, hunkering down for the brutal winter ahead, taking all their pills at the right time, drinking their oxtail soup, trying to stop themselves from dying somehow, when the scandal blew up and suddenly it seemed that they mightn't have to wait that long after all.

Could it be that the poor ould fellas were about to get a lucky break? Could it possibly be?

With mounting excitement, they watched the special RTÉ

Presidents of Ireland they like

Douglas Hyde
Seán T. O'Kelly
Éamon de Valera
Erskine Childers
Cearbhall Ó Dálaigh
Patrick Hillery

He died in his office...

broadcast of Leader's Questions in the House, grateful to have a programme on in the afternoon with men in it for once. And no ordinary programme either, but a programme that could change their lives, or whatever was left of their lives.

Of course, they were disappointed that the government might fall because of a "dig-out" that Bertie got, from what must have been a very big hole, and not because of the smoking ban. Why were Fianna Fáil's "partners in government", the Progressive Democrats, so upset about a few quid that changed hands about fifteen years ago when it doesn't seem to matter to them at all that a genuinely bad thing was done by this government when it brought in the smoking ban?

Ultimately, it didn't really matter to the poor ould fellas how Bertie and his government went down, as long as they went down while the poor ould fellas were still around to enjoy it. But still ... all this bullshit about Bertie's house and Bertie's wife and Bertie sleeping in his office and Bertie's bank account that never was ... who gives a fiddler's when there are serious crimes against humanity to be addressed?

The same Bertie is particularly culpable for the neglect of the poor ould fellas because a man in his situation should be able to empathise with them more than most – like Bertie, it's a long time since the poor ould fellas had a wife to look after them; they too have lived the lonely bachelor existence, finding release only in the occasional football match, if not quite in the executive lounges of Old Trafford after a journey by private jet; and they too have operated for a long time without a bank account, because they have no frigging money.

And any "savings" they might have accumulated over the years are best kept around the house to throw to burglars, in the hope that the bit of cash in hand might persuade the drug-addled youths not to break the poor ould fella's skull with a lump hammer.

So Bertie had his troubles but they involved him getting big wodges of money from "the lads" – which is the sort of trouble the poor ould fellas could live with, all things considered.

Of course, it was the Tribunal from which these "revelations" emerged, and of course the poor ould fellas can often be found up there in Dublin Castle, trying to kill the day by listening to long-winded accounts of who was getting what from whom while the poor ould fellas were getting bugger all from anyone.

Yes, Bertie may have cribbed about having to expose himself to the Tribunal and about leaks, but explaining where all these "moneys" came from is perhaps not quite as annoying as having no "moneys" at all after a lifetime of honest toil.

And as for leaks – all sorts of gunk has been leaking out of the poor ould fellas, from every orifice, for years. The world just looks away …

So his government may have turned its back on the poor ould fellas, but surprisingly soon, Bertie himself will know what it's like to be a poor ould fella himself.

He will know rejection and frustration and humiliation and defeat.

And for this crucial week, with Bertie under the gun, it was the fervent wish of the poor ould fellas that he would know these things on an election night in November rather than May.

But it all drifted away from them, in a haze of bullshit, the poor ould fellas disappointed once more as they listened to Bertiespeak such as this: "I didn't tell the present Tánaiste about Michael Wall and I didn't see what. I didn't see, he didn't want to know that either of who I bought my house from. In so far as it's painted a connection now that Michael Wall was somebody who was at the Manchester function. Well he wasn't at the Manchester function. Yes, yes but he was not a donor, he was not, and that's the fact."

These were perhaps the last words heard by certain poor

US Presidents they like

Gerald Ford (a decent man)
JFK

Billy Kierans actually met him when he was over...

ould fellas in this life. Because all week their hearts were beating a little faster, but their hearts aren't meant to do that, except under proper medical supervision. The excitement of that week's skullduggery, that little rush of hope, was just too much for some of the poor buggers. And so they croaked.

While other men might hear fine words spoken in Latin at the pass over to the other side, all the poor ould fellas could hear, before they departed this cruel world, was the gibberish of Bertie Ahern.

But there were many more of them out there who would keep on living somehow, till May 2007 at least, their rheumy old eyes fixed even more firmly on the prize.

The General Election of 2007 – Part III

They had tried hard to take the good out of it for the poor ould fellas. They had spent millions, indeed they had wasted millions, on electronic voting machines which would have deprived the poor ould fellas of one of the last earthly pleasures known to them, that of participating in the democratic process in the old-style system of proportional representation.

It is a pleasure rarely indulged, and the very infrequency of an election made it something for the poor ould fellas to savour. But not any more.

The poor ould fellas who voted in the election of 2007 would be the last of the poor ould fellas to partake of this modest enjoyment. At least, that is the plan conceived by the geniuses who brought in the voting machines in the first place, only to find that they couldn't use them.

And when they tried using them during the last election in a few test cases, everyone hated them. Which did nothing to discourage the advocates of electronic voting, who feel that the system is innately better.

But it is not innately better. As the poor ould fellas knew, before anyone else knew, it is innately worse. It is, in short, bullshit. But does it not provide a quick result, thus saving time which might otherwise be wasted counting votes by hand?

In response to this, the poor ould fellas would reason that the counting of votes can be quite interesting in a close contest. And on the whole, if something is interesting it is better if it lasts a long time, rather than a short time. In this way, there is more enjoyment to be had, and human beings tend to regard enjoyment as a good thing.

This would be the thinking of the poor ould fellas if anyone bothered to ask them, but of course nobody did.

In fact, many poor ould fellas were somewhat surprised when they limped up to the polling station to find that they still actually had the vote. And that their vote was still worth the same as the vote of an able-bodied person, a person who matters.

But despite the obstacles they would encounter on the day, they were determined to vote against the government which had destroyed the Irish pub and tolerated all the other bullshit. Some poor ould fellas even voted more than once, dragging themselves to another polling booth to use the dead brother's vote, because it's what he would have wanted.

Of course they had followed the debates during the campaign on a wide range of issues – indeed almost every issue imaginable was raised, from the stamp duty on Bertie's rented house to all that terrible, terrible bullshit about "communities", but strangely, there was very little about the poor ould fellas. By "very little" here, I mean to say nothing.

But they would have their say on 24 May. They had been living for this day, if "living" is not putting it too strongly.

And so on this day, one by one, they emerged into the

harsh light of summer. One by one, they made this last effort, dragging themselves down to the polling stations, marking the paper 1, 2, 3, all the way down, for old time's sake and for spite.

One by one, they put the ballot paper into the box for the last time.

And then, one by one, they went home.

And by the time they had put the kettle on to warm themselves up for what they knew would be their last election special, they were philosophical. They were resigned to the fact that, whoever got elected, the smoking ban and all the other bullshit was going to stay. So in that sense, they had stayed alive in vain. Indeed, in many other senses, they had stayed alive in vain.

But as they threw a splash of whiskey into the mug of tea, settling in for the long night, they told themselves that Minister Micheál Martin was in for a rude awakening in Cork – in fact he was elected with about fourteen quotas. And they told themselves that Bertie wouldn't get away with it – in fact he had been declared duly elected *before* the polls had closed.

They had voted for change, the only sort of change they can abide – namely, change back to what things were like in the first place.

They were pissing in the wind.

THE MODERN
WORLD

Guinness and Trousers – Things that Work

Reporters at the tribunals have noted the poignant scene which takes place in the late afternoon, an exodus of poor ould fellas shuffling away from Dublin Castle to get the bus home while the bus pass is still valid. It is poignant that these men are regarded as a nuisance during the rush-hour, and doubly poignant that the tribunals are one of the few recreations left open to them, where they can learn in excruciating detail how the country was carved up while they were out working for a living.

And another thing as regards our abysmal treatment of the poor ould fellas – it diminishes us all. These men are a vital natural resource who are treated as if they were a waste of space, surplus to requirements. They have amassed much wisdom along the way, which they would dispense for free if anyone could be bothered to talk to them. They could have advised Guinness, for example, that the introduction of low-alcohol stout will probably be about as successful as all the other efforts to introduce variations on the stout theme, such as Guinness Light.

The poor ould fellas know that a pint of stout is a bit like a pair of trousers. The original trousers concept is still the best, a garment that you put your two legs into and fasten at the top. It doesn't need to change in any way – a man can wear trousers all his life and never ask himself if he might prefer to be wearing a sari instead, like the young Beckham.

So to suggest to a poor ould fella that he might make the change to low-alcohol Guinness is like suggesting that he might enjoy wearing a sari as he sits at home alone, smoking his last few cigarettes and, of course, missing the company in the pub, where he would be drinking traditional draught Guinness and nothing but traditional draught Guinness, the only thing that's permanent in this world.

They said that low-alcohol Guinness would be "less challenging". But if they'd asked the poor ould fellas about this, they'd have realised that, over the years, a man might reject a pint of Guinness because it is badly pulled or for some such obscure technical reason, but the only circumstances in which he will find it too "challenging" is when he has consumed about twenty-four pints already and he just can't take any more.

Otherwise, you can drink pints all your life and find it no more challenging than remembering to put your trousers on before you leave the house. As the poor ould fellas with their hard-won wisdom could tell the marketing men, trousers and Guinness are things that just work somehow, the way that poor ould fellas drinking and smoking in the pub used to work, the way that Johnny McEvoy on afternoon TV used to work.

And even young people know this, as they complain that you have to drink twice as much low-alcohol Guinness to

have the desired effect. This scuppers the notion that young people want a different type of Guinness because they associate the classic pint with poor ould fellas. Most likely, they are unaware that such a thing as a poor ould fella even exists, except in sepia-tinged picture postcards.

And the more we treat the poor ould fellas as non-persons, the more we miss their astute observations on life, and especially on stout. As a poor ould fella once told me, contemplating a glass of the new "extra cold" porter, "you'd need fuckin' gloves for that".

He said that change was his enemy, and how right he was.

And if you told him that the pregnant Gwyneth Paltrow was seen drinking Guinness because Guinness is good for you, he'd wonder where you'd been for the last fifty years.

These men have known things all their lives that Gwyneth Paltrow only discovered last month.

Yet they are the pariahs of the new Ireland, where supposedly smart guys come to them and say, "Old-timer, you know the Guinness you've been drinking for sixty-eight years, the grandest drink in the history of the world? Well, we've got a different version of it here for the new Ireland."

For the birds, sonny, for the birds.

The Poor Ould Fella's Kitchen Cupboard

UNLIKELY TO HAVE:

Garlic, Pasta,
"Still" water, Cumin,
Oregano, Ginger,
Nutmeg, Chilli powder,
Baby rocket leaves,
Parma ham, Mozzarella
cheese, Extra virgin
olive oil.

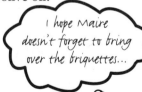

I hope Maire doesn't forget to bring over the briquettes...

LIKELY TO HAVE:

Tin of baked beans,
Sugar, Bisto, 7 Up,
MiWadi (where
available),
Oxtail soup
(several packets of),
Tin of peas
(processed),
Cream crackers,
Beef stock cubes,
Tomato sauce,
Brown sauce,
Calvita cheese
(with the girl on the
packet), Ginger-nut
biscuits, Box of
Cadbury's Roses,
Tea, Salt,
Mazzola cooking oil.

Google My Arse

Was it an illusion or did we actually see an item on the RTÉ news one evening in 2006 about senior citizens in Meath having a great time discovering the Internet? Are we seriously to deduce from this that there is light at the end of the tunnel for our friends, the poor ould fellas? Or was it just another cruel mirage?

Certainly, the pictures told a happy story of elderly men and women expanding their horizons, discovering the myriad uses of the Internet. But we didn't see any sign there of what we would describe as a poor ould fella, in the true sense of the words.

No, we don't think this would be for them. No, we can't see them getting a big rush of excitement when they're told that this is a really handy way of booking flights. We can't see them getting a buzz when they're introduced to Google, the Internet search engine.

In fact, they would be looking at this RTÉ item on a small black-and-white television in the isolated shack which they share with a poor ould dog called Mick, and in all likelihood they'd be saying to themselves: "Google ... my ... arse."

You see, these are not the sort of men who feel that their lives would be greatly improved if only they could communicate more with other people, either in real life or on the World Wide Web. As far as they're concerned, and quite rightly too, their communicating days are over. They've spent the last seventy-five years communicating and they feel that they're entitled to a rest from all that.

If the poor ould fellas haven't taken to the mobile phone, they'll hardly find much to divert them in an Internet chatroom. Though they are encouraged by members of the so-called "caring" professions to possess a mobile phone, if only to dial 999 for the ambulance, they have tended to resist its manifold charms – not for them, either, the BlackBerry. And somehow they have resisted that massive David Beckham campaign mounted by Vodafone because, for some strange reason, the poor ould fellas couldn't quite see the point of taking pictures of themselves and sending them down the phone to other poor ould fellas.

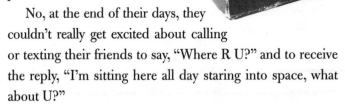

No, at the end of their days, they couldn't really get excited about calling or texting their friends to say, "Where R U?" and to receive the reply, "I'm sitting here all day staring into space, what about U?"

There is just one form of meaningful communication which they desire, but of course it is denied to them.

For this form of communication to take place, they'd need to be sitting in a bar, not dipping biscuits into their tea in some too-bright day-care centre filled with suspiciously cheerful people showing them how to use a laptop computer. They'd need a friendly barman who understands a few simple hand-signals and who responds by bringing them a pint of stout and a packet of smokes to be consumed by the poor ould fellas on the premises, as nature intended it.

Alas, it will never happen. Never again in their lifetimes will they savour this, the one true pleasure that was left to them.

And if well-meaning individuals think that surfing the net will ever be an adequate substitute for supping porter and smoking fags, I'm afraid they are sadly deluded.

Nor would the poor ould fellas be greatly tempted by the Internet as a means of doing "research". With some justification, at this stage they feel that they know enough.

They know too much, if truth be told. And they've seen too much to be overly impressed by some well-meaning lady showing them how to book a cheap hotel room in Sardinia for a holiday which they have no intention of having.

Would it kill the day for them? Would looking into a screen for no reason help to pass those empty hours? Perhaps, but there's a far, far better way of killing the day, which satisfied all the earthly needs of the poor ould fellas until Minister Micheál Martin effectively abolished it.

Instead, they are invited to discover the Internet so that they can find out more about all the diseases they have, these men who wouldn't even tell the doctor what was wrong with them, and wouldn't want the doctor to tell them either. Which may seem unreasonable to various busybodies, but these men knew a time when people guarded their privacy.

And is this supposed to be a better time, now that you can whip out a credit card and buy yourself a heap of Internet porn? Some might say that the Internet porn would certainly kill the day for the poor ould fellas, because they would look at it and in all likelihood they would drop dead, leaving Mick the dog to roam around the countryside for about fourteen days, looking for assistance.

But it's not a runner anyway, because poor ould fellas don't have credit cards.

Arguably, they'd enjoy the Internet gambling, if anyone would show them how to operate it. Which they wouldn't, for fear the poor ould fellas might actually enjoy themselves. And again, a poor ould fella with a credit card is a creature so rare and exotic he'd probably end up being filmed by David Attenborough.

So that's that then.

What to buy them on their Birthday

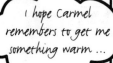

The Quiet Man on DVD
(even though they don't have
anything to play it on)

Cadbury's Roses

Whiskey

Socks

Johnny McEvoy CD
(even though they don't have
anything to play it on)

Calendar of local GAA team

What not to buy them on their Birthday

U2's latest album

Anything "pour homme"

A voucher for a weekend at a spa

A book by Lynne Truss

Nivea for Men Aftershave Balm

A framed print or painting

Aromatic candles

Anything from the *Irish Times* Collection

"Fun" socks

Coffee percolator

Boxed set of *The West Wing*

Nicholas Mosse pottery

The Hovel that is Worth a Million

On the whole, the poor ould fellas haven't been paying much attention to Ireland's property boom. Despite *The Irish Times'* desire to reach out to readers beyond the Pale and introduce them to a better way of life, when the good people at the Paper of Record are compiling the famous Thursday property supplement, the poor ould fellas are not exactly uppermost in their thoughts.

And this is probably understandable, on strictly commercial grounds.

After all, the poor ould fellas are not exactly rushing out on Thursday morning with a fierce urge to be first in the queue when the newsagent cuts open *The Irish Times*. In fact, they're not exactly rushing out any other morning either to grab their copy of the Paper of Record, and indeed, they haven't taken a paper with any regularity since the *Sunday Press* and the *Evening Press* and the *Irish Press* ceased publication towards the end of the last century.

They still take the *Sunday World* occasionally, because Con Houlihan writes a column in it, because it has stories about the criminals who will soon be visiting the poor ould fellas to rob them and perhaps to bludgeon them to death, and because the *Sunday World* has the best pictures. Usually

if the other papers have a picture of the scenes of devastation in Nairobi after a car bomb, the *Sunday World* will have a picture of a nice girl in a bathing costume who just wants to say "hello" – an editorial choice which the poor ould fellas find easier on the nerves and which, in extreme cases, may even give them the horn.

So the poor ould fellas would not be part of the ABC1 demographic which takes *The Irish Times* not so much as a daily paper but as a quasi-religious rite. And they certainly wouldn't be bumping up the sales on Thursday, when the property section unveils its many treasures.

Languishing as they do in some demographic which hardly even registers on the scale – would they be in the XYZ26 category? – the poor ould fellas wouldn't be sitting there sipping their morning coffee and drooling over the interior of some Shrewsbury Road mansion which has been sold by a High Court judge to some computer billionaire for €46 million.

They wouldn't be gasping at the fabulous light-filled extension which has turned an artisan's cottage in Ringsend into a €4 million gem. And they wouldn't be rushing out to buy *VIP* magazine because it has pictures of Keith Duffy relaxing in his fabulous new light-filled conservatory.

In fact, they're generally put off by all this "light" business. They see Duncan Stewart on the telly, and Duncan seems to be totally obsessed with light. "Oh, the light is wonderful here!" he says to some smashing couple who have designed and built their own house, because they're great.

"Oh, it's all so bright, since you put in the skylights," he enthuses. To the poor ould fellas, Duncan seems so keen on the light he would prefer if there was no roof at all on the house to let in more light, and more light, and even more frigging light.

The poor ould fellas, by contrast, are wary of all that light. They find it soothing to sit inside on a dazzling summer's day with the curtains drawn, avoiding the damaging rays of the sun and the exhausting heat.

So they wouldn't be getting the horn looking at a lovely *Irish Times* picture of the spectacular conservatory which was personally designed by a member of the rock band Def Leppard to suit his unique sunbathing requirements and which has made his residence on Killiney Hill even more valuable, if that is possible.

No, the poor ould fellas wouldn't be palpitating at the sight of that, getting on the blower to Sherry Fitzgerald to arrange a viewing.

You certainly don't see too many poor ould fellas sauntering through the auction rooms, perusing the catalogue with a knowing air, exuding an air of mystery and possibly wearing a cravat, opening the bidding at a modest €14 million for Eddie Irvine's old place.

That wouldn't be their style at all.

But while they wouldn't be paying much attention to Ireland's property boom, Ireland's property boom has certainly been paying attention to them.

It has not escaped the attention of the property hounds that many poor ould fellas just happen to live in areas of outstanding natural beauty. And while their hovels might be described in *The Irish Times* as "full of character" and "offering loads of exciting potential for restoration", there's no doubt that, as regards location, location and location, the poor ould fellas have got it made.

At least in the shrunken universe inhabited by the estate agent, they've got it made.

In their own shrunken universe, the poor ould fellas themselves don't see it like that in the slightest.

A poor ould fella may be fiercely attached to the land, but

you wouldn't find him ambling across the property admiring the scenery. You wouldn't find him setting up an easel in a field and doing a bit of landscape painting as an artistic and a therapeutic exercise.

When he looks at the area of outstanding natural beauty in which he resides, he does not see a vision of paradise. Instead he sees a spot over yonder where he pulled a bullock out of a drain, or he sees a spot in the far field where he got a kick from a mad horse that broke his jaw, which still pains him because it has never fully healed, or he sees several spots where they had to dig a grave and bury a poor ould dog called Mick.

And anyway, being fiercely attached to the land means that he has no intention of selling it to the highest bidder and moving ... where? To a four-bedroomed detached residence in a leafy suburb?

A long-lost relative may come calling, a nephew, perhaps, with an eye for the main chance.

Obviously the poor ould fella won't recognise him, because the nephew was a small boy when he last saw him, and there has been no communication between them since the nephew, then aged six, scrawled his name on a postcard which was sent to the poor ould fella from the Canaries: "Having a wonderful time, wish you were here" – which the poor ould fella figured was just taking the piss.

Anyway, the nephew is now a man on the make, looking for a piece of the poor ould fella's estate, but the poor ould fella, assuming that he hasn't slipped into the latter stages of helpless dementia, is having none of it.

What's in their pockets

Handkerchief
Penknife
Loose change
Key to the house
Key to the shed (attached
to Padre Pio
keyring/ bottle opener)
Tablets
Fox's Glacier Mints
Lottery scratch card
Blackberries (wrapped in handkerchief)

What's not in their pockets

Calculator
Mobile phone
iPod mini
Mini Filofax
"BlackBerry"

I must get
another set of keys
cut for the nurse ...

In fact, he too can take the piss, pretending he is deafer than he actually is, driving the nephew increasingly bonkers, roaring at the poor ould fella and still getting all the wrong answers.

Defeated, the nephew may actually offer to pay a fair market price for the hovel to "keep it in the family".

And this might have its attractions, on paper, but it wouldn't really suit the poor ould fellas, who are opposed to change of almost any kind, let alone a change of such enormity.

Could they perhaps be tempted by a million euro, which could buy them either another hovel in another area of out-standing natural beauty or an excellent apartment in Bulgaria with enough money to live on, Bulgaria-style, for the rest of their lives?

And if they tire of Bulgaria, could they eventually sell the apartment in Bulgaria for one-tenth of the price they paid for it and return to their native place to take up residence in the County Home?

Certainly, such offers have been made to them from time to time. They have heard the Mercedes purring down the lane, and they have drawn the curtains, thinking that it might well be an estate agent, because the burglars tend to use Hiace vans.

Cowering within, they can hear the estate agent with his South Dublin twang. "I have a vurry attractive offer to make to you, my good man," the agent drawls.

And the poor ould fella has to sit there for as long as it takes, listening to the buggers going around the back, rattling the bars on the windows, while Mick the dog stays inside, barking his head off. Should the poor ould fella just let Mick loose on the buggers? No, they'd only put in a claim for compo and Mick might end up getting the bullet.

"I can come back later, sir, if that suits you better," the agent bawls through the letter-box, while the poor ould fella hides.

And eventually he goes away, no doubt to annoy some other poor ould fella whose hovel he plans to bulldoze within two minutes of the papers being signed ... If only he could bulldoze it now, and the poor ould fella within ... Yes, if only all the poor ould fellas could somehow be bulldozed and replaced by reasonable people who want to do business ...

But sometimes the fellow in the Mercedes gets lucky and the poor ould fella is trapped, intercepted as he comes out of the henhouse just yards from the sanctuary of his home, which is full of character and offers loads of exciting potential for restoration.

Then he has to listen to the bullshit. He'll never actually let the fellow into the house, but he'll have to stand there mortified as the fellow in the expensive suit with the waft of eau de cologne tells him that he might have much to gain from "downsizing".

Of course, it would be nice to have a few hundred thousand left over after "downsizing" to a new house in an estate on the outskirts of Nenagh with all mod cons. But no poor ould fella wants to be downsizing at this stage of his life.

And the situation may be further complicated by the fact that there may be two poor ould fellas involved, not just the one. It is not unknown for two poor ould fellas, usually brothers, to share the same dilapidated living space, with all the potential for acrimony that this implies.

Indeed, we have heard of one particularly chilling case from the midlands of a poor ould fella who did all the cooking for himself and the other poor ould fella. Though they hadn't exchanged a word for years, due to some ancient bitterness, "the biha dinner" still had to be made and consumed in terrible silence.

So alienated had they become from one another that the poor ould fella who did the cooking failed to notice that the other poor ould fella had died. He had died, but he was still propped up in the chair in what the other poor ould fella presumed was some sort of a relatively harmless coma. For at least two days, the old routine was observed, with one poor ould fella putting "the biha dinner" in front of the other poor ould fella and neither of them talking.

Life went on as usual, if you discount the minor detail that one of them wasn't actually alive any more.

So if moving house is the most stressful thing that any normal, healthy person can do, how much more stressful might it be for the poor ould fellas? At the end of their days, ideally the only house they will move to is the house with no windows on Boot Hill.

But withal, they are not completely excluded from enjoying the benefits of the property market.

Their homes may be worth a million to them, in theory only. But to send an estate agent back up the road to Dublin with his tail between his legs is a pleasure beyond price.

Bullshit!!!

Draconian drink-driving laws
Smoking ban in pubs
Political correctness
Paris Hilton
Fancy salt and pepper shakers
iPods
Stem-cell research
Cloning
Live Aid
"The Theatre"

The Carvery Lunch

It was just another ad on the radio, this ad which pointed out that there are great laughs to be had down the pub with your pals, and if you want to partake of all this merriment, you should get yourself down there one of these nights.

It was just another ad on the radio and no one passed any remarks on it. No one, that is, apart from the last surviving members of a forgotten tribe which we call the poor ould fellas.

When the poor ould fellas heard this ad on the wireless, they knew straight away what they were hearing and what it meant.

It meant the end of a way of life, of a civilisation that had prospered and which most of the Irish had assumed would go on forever but which, within a few short years, had all but vanished from the face of the earth.

And the fact that so few of us saw this coming, or gave a damn about it while it was happening right in front of us, was further proof – if proof were needed – that indeed we were in the presence of an awesome phenomenon in Irish history. We were looking at nothing less than the death of the Irish pub.

What other interpretation could be placed on this truly extraordinary thing, an ad for pubs on Irish radio? Since when did the Irish have to be inveigled into a night's drinking by a twee little sketch dreamed up by some arsehole in an ad agency? How in the name of God had it come to this?

Some will point to sociological and lifestyle factors and other such bullshit, but the poor ould fellas saw the writing on the wall several years ago when pubs decided, in their wisdom, to stop being pubs.

Yes, that would explain it. That's what the poor ould fellas saw – pubs which stopped being pubs. Certainly they had stopped being pubs in the true sense of the word, and towards the end, they weren't pubs in any sense of the word.

A pub, for thousands of years, was a place in which men drank. Yes, that would be a pretty fair description of a pub. A place in which alcoholic drink was served to men, and occasionally women, but mostly men.

Indeed, most women were quite happy to stay away from the pub, for all sorts of reasons, not least because it might involve an encounter with a poor ould fella in his natural habitat – then, as now, poor ould fellas were treated with a certain lofty disdain but, crucially, back then they at least had a natural habitat, a place in which they could take refuge, where they could go for some small measure of consolation in an otherwise hostile world.

That's how it worked, and for a long time it worked very well.

Especially in Ireland.

So much so that certain men brought the concept of the "Irish pub" to other lands, with an Irish pub now to be found in every city in the world. Which makes most of the Irish proud when they go abroad, but which to the poor ould fellas is bullshit of the most heinous kind. And they don't need to go abroad to know that.

Bullshit, complete and utter bullshit, for the very obvious reason that there are virtually no Irish pubs left in Ireland any more, so what are these yokes masquerading as Irish pubs in Germany and France? Bullshit is what they are.

They are bullshit heaped upon layers of bullshit which began some years ago when pubs stopped being pubs and started introducing things like coffee and food. At first it was just the odd package of peanuts or maybe a metallic bowl of oxtail soup and a ham sandwich.

But it was the principle of the thing that rankled with the poor ould fellas.

Mostly they refused to indulge in any of this bullshit, though in an emergency they might be persuaded to drink a bowl of oxtail soup – but only in an emergency.

Now there would be fellows wearing cravats coming in for a cup of coffee and a sandwich where once men drank porter. And whiskey. But mainly porter.

Gradually the pubs became lounge bars with all sorts of eating and drinking and bands that would blow your head off in the lounge, while the poor ould fellas were consigned to the bar to drink whiskey and porter, as they had been doing since time immemorial.

They knew deep down that their days were numbered, that soon the wall would be coming down and the whole pub would be given over to all that other racket. All that eating, defined for the poor ould fellas by the dreaded words "carvery lunch".

Carve those words, indeed, on the hearts of the poor ould fellas.

Because most days now in pubs, instead of men drinking, you see a long queue of punters holding trays, filing past this stainless-steel counter where there's a fellow dressed as a chef cutting slices of roast beef off a succulent joint, then scooping onto a plate the potatoes and two veg, which the carvery lunch comprises.

Where in this dismal scene is there a place for the poor ould fellas?

There is no place for them here, obviously. Perhaps, indeed, that was the whole point of the exercise, a systematic process of annihilation, the final act of which was the smoking ban.

Oh yes, there's no smoke to be found in the pubs now either, because it's not right to have punters eating the carvery lunch in a smoky environment, is it?

Funny, it never occurred to anyone that maybe it wasn't right to have poor ould fellas trying to drink and smoke with a fucking carvery lunch going on all around them, but that's the way the world is going.

It's a world, it must be said, that is increasingly ruled by women. And as Benny Hill so rightly pointed out in "Ernie", a woman's needs are manifold.

To the poor ould fellas it is abundantly clear that none of this destruction could have happened without the women. It is they, more than anyone else, who wanted pubs to stop

being pubs and to be more airy and bright and family friendly and all that bullshit, which is all very fine if you're running
Butlins but not if men are trying to sell drink to other
men, as they have done since the time of Christ, and even
before that.

Moreover, as pubs go out of business as surely as night
follows day, the poor ould fellas can see through all this lifestyle
and sociology bullshit to the heart of the matter. The reason
that men are no longer going to the pub to drink fourteen
or fifteen quiet pints of porter, as they have
traditionally done, is that the women won't
let them.

They used to let them, but they won't
let them any more.

Because the women wear the
trousers now.

And item one on their agenda was the ruination and effectively the abolition of the things that men enjoyed above all others – namely, drinking pints and smoking fags.

Slowly, inexorably, the idea of a place just for drinking pints became socially unacceptable, or at least socially unacceptable to the women and to certain men who carry on like women, the New Men as they are called, recognised at first sight by the poor ould fellas as their natural enemy.

Together the women and the New Men relentlessly attacked and ridiculed the time-honoured custom of the poor ould fellas, that of drinking pints in public bars. And after that, the idea of a place where you could be smoking fags as well as drinking pints became equally unacceptable both to the women and to men like Minister Micheál Martin, who took it upon himself to do the dirty deed – the killer blow that is the smoking ban, but just the last of many other blows, which began when that first sip of coffee and that first sup of soup were consumed on licensed premises by men who did not know what they were starting.

And then came the bottled water, still or sparkling.

Most poor ould fellas can tell you exactly where they were when they saw that first bottle of sparkling Ballygowan being offered for sale in a public house – they were in that public house. And they were laughing out loud, a rare enough sound in modern Ireland where there is so little to amuse them. But this ... this was funny, this bottle of water that the barman was selling – actually looking for money in exchange for water.

And the funniest part of it all was that eejits soon started putting their hands in their pockets and buying the water. And thinking they were great fellas, to be drinking bubbly water like some sort of a Frenchman.

But at least the bubbly water had bubbles in it. The still water had nothing in it except water, and it was totally beyond the comprehension of the poor ould fellas that Irishmen, and of course Irishwomen, would actually pay a pound for still water because it was in a bottle.

In fact, for the poor ould fellas, one of the great mysteries of the age is this whole water obsession which has gripped the Irish, who can now be seen constantly slugging from a bottle of water, not just in the pub, but even when they're walking down the street.

Were they all parched for the last five million years, until the day that Ballygowan was invented?

Anyway, it's all over now.

They brought in their bottles of still water and bubbly water and their carvery lunch, thinking they were smart, trying to please the women, and they end up doing the unthinkable, paying for an ad on the radio for pubs – surely the last resort of desperate men.

They forced out the poor ould fellas who had sustained them for generations. Yes, the poor ould fellas are all gone now and they won't be coming back. Because those places are all gone too where men could be at ease with themselves and with other men, thinking that the day would never come when they would arrive up to the bar and be presented with, of all things, a menu.

There's a place for a menu and that place is called a restaurant.

Not that the poor ould fellas would have much use for a menu in any setting.

They don't do lunch.

At the Lower End of Expectations

Let us look closely at this extract from the annual statement of the Paddy Power organisation: "The gross win percentage was at the lower end of expectations, or modestly below the weighted average mid-point of the guided ranges."

What does this mean? It means, I think, that some new standard has been set for bullshit everywhere. And that the world has been made just that little less comprehensible to the poor ould fellas.

The part about the "gross win percentage being at the lower end of expectations" is all right. In fact, it is probably good news for the poor ould fellas, as, in plain English, it means that Paddy Power didn't make as much money as he expected to make last year. And this would please the poor ould fellas, who enjoy a bet and who regard the likes of Paddy Power and all the other betting corporations as their natural enemy. It would suggest that there is some sort of divine justice at work, though of course the poor ould fellas realise, after a moment's reflection, that there isn't.

They could also understand the sentiment, as their whole lives tend to be lived "at the lower end of expectations". In fact, over time their expectations have been lowered to such an extent you could say they have no expectations at all,

except that everything will turn out bad.

But the second part of the statement would have no meaning at all to any normal punter, and certainly not to the poor ould fellas.

Clearly the "weighted average mid-point of the guided ranges" is some sort of economic bullshit and, like so much in this world, it is quite unnecessary and utterly confusing.

And this, after all, is an area in which the poor ould fellas have some expertise. They were backing horses for about fifty years before Paddy Power got it into his head that you could make a gross win percentage from the gaming industry that was modestly above the weighted average mid-point of the guided ranges.

And in that time they saw some changes, which were all supposedly for the good, but of course not for the good of the poor ould fellas. Time was when a man would enter a bookie's office which was situated down a side street in the wrong part of town and there, in the most rudimentary conditions, he would place a bet on a horse. Or maybe a dog. But most likely a horse.

He would not be given the option of betting on tennis or darts or motor-racing or American football, and this was probably a good thing. He would not be offered odds on who would score the first goal for Arsenal, what the score would be at half-time and full-time and the number of corners in the match. And this was definitely a good thing.

He would not turn on his wireless to hear some gas character from Paddy Power telling his RTÉ host about various "fun bets" they are offering the punters, and the RTÉ host laughing his head off while Paddy Power gets loads of free advertising for gems such as this: Jack Charlton is 100/1 to become the next president of Ireland – isn't that just hilarious? And Bertie Ahern is 50/1 to become the next manager of The Dubs – could anything be funnier than that?

No, the poor ould fella was spared such comedy classics back in the day.

Nor could he watch the racing or the dogs live on a bank of screens, making him feel like some big player on the floor of a stock exchange for men with no money.

No, all he could do was have his bet and maybe listen to some dreary commentary dribbling through a battered speaker, a service which was probably illegal but what the hell? Nobody cared enough to close it all down, because the respectable classes were largely unaffected by it.

And the poor ould fellas weren't complaining, in fact they were quite happy with the situation, because there was nothing wrong with it. And it worked.

At least it worked for them.

Did they need tea- and coffee-machines and water-coolers? No, if they needed such things, they would go either to a café or a bad pub.

Did they need soft seats and carpets? No, such things would only encourage them to relax and to lose more money.

Did they need toilets? No, they did not need toilets, nor did it ever cross their minds that such things might be provided. Women need toilets; men just need to bet.

But eventually they got all these creature comforts anyway, which they never asked for and didn't need. They got the free "still water" and the colour co-ordination.

But they lost something they would always want and would desperately need. They lost the right to smoke, to suck on a Harry Wragg to ease their poor nerves as they listened to the racing.

Indeed, once the respectable classes had completed the job of sanitising the betting industry, with their carpets and their toilets, it seemed almost normal not to be allowed to smoke in a betting office, where once it would have seemed like the strangest scene imaginable and rightly so.

The smoke-filled betting office always looked right. The sight of men standing outside a betting office smoking while the horses are inside running does not look right.

But then, if your main concern is that the gross win percentage is at the higher end of expectations, or considerably above the weighted average mid-point of the guided ranges, what do you care about such things?

And of course the level of service, while apparently more friendly and efficient, is exposed for what it is by the poor ould fellas, especially after they've had a few bottles of porter

Even more Bullshit!!!

Virtual racing
Kebabs
Internet cafés
Karaoke
Pasta
Astrology
Wine
Newspapers with free CDs
Barbecues
Electronic voting
Counselling
Homeopathy

Why would you want to cook something in the garden?

and their writing on the dockets is perhaps not as crystal clear as it might be.

Time was when the contrary old bastard behind the counter, for all his faults, would always be able to read the squiggles of the poor ould fella and pay out accordingly.

Now the punter is kept waiting by some young one wearing a company uniform who starts a debate on the matter, right there in the shop. She calls for the manager, the two of them scrutinising the hieroglyphics of the poor ould fella, basically calling him a liar, implying that he's pulling a fast one on the great corporation in whose fine emporium he is enjoying this unique gaming experience.

This would all be avoidable if the poor ould fellas could sit at home with a laptop computer, having opened an online-betting account. But one of the few innovations which might actually improve the lives of the poor ould fellas is denied to them, for a variety of reasons. Online betting came too late for them, really. It would just take too long to conquer their perfectly justified fear of the laptop and of computer science in general, and they couldn't afford it anyway. And even if they could, they would need a credit card to start betting. And while American Express and Mastercard provide an excellent service in many ways, they are not exactly renowned for sending out plastic to poor ould fellas for gambling purposes.

No, the credit rating of the poor ould fellas would not be the best.

Nor do they have the other option which was available to

them in better days – that of actually going to the races, of "letting their lugs back", as the saying goes.

The Galway Races in particular were much loved by the poor ould fellas, who could usually rely on a neighbour to give them a lift there and back. In fact, often out of simple deference to the older man, the neighbour would insist that the poor ould fella sat in the front seat, while his own wife or other family members sat in the back.

The poor ould fellas would reciprocate by giving the younger ones money for sweets, a tradition which could last until the young ones were well into their thirties. And he would mark their cards, because no one knew racing like the poor ould fellas knew it.

But it's increasingly rare now to see a poor ould fella getting his lift, sitting in the front seat wearing his hat or his cap at all times. People love their cars now more than they love their poor ould neighbours – they're afraid that they'll want to smoke or that they'll give off these strange ould-fella odours which will never quite go away. They're afraid, basically, that it might be any trouble.

And the poor ould fellas are put off, anyway, by what Galway has become, a place for the big-swinging-mickeys, the punters landing in their helicopters, the arseholes gathering in their tents to stroke each other while they talk about their gross win percentage, which is at the higher end of expectations.

Those guys can fool all the people all the time. All the people, that is, except a small and diminishing minority watching the week's racing at home on the telly they bought when they backed the winner of the Galway Plate in 1968, watching Ted Walsh on RTÉ and remembering the days when they would go to Galway and let their lugs back.

Food they like

Sausages
Rashers
Eggs
Toast
Stew
Butter
Beans

Food they don't like

Butter beans   Cannelloni
Vegetable lasagne   Chinese
Chilli con carne   Thai
Hummus   Indian
Chicken Maryland

The Poor Ould Fella who Ate the Money

Before we relate the true story of the poor ould fella who ate the money, we should look at the overall position of the poor ould fellas in relation to the phenomenon of modern food.

It is a position best summed up by a recent vignette in which a poor ould fella is sitting down in a hotel restaurant having the bit of grub after the funeral of another poor ould fella. And the waitress comes along and says to him, "Would you like a slice of carrot cake, sir?" And the poor ould fella says, "If it's all the same to you, Deirdre, I'll just have a bottle of stout."

Yes, as he looks back on his long, long life, a poor ould fella may have many regrets, but he will shed no tears about the fact that he has lived all that time and never once tried a slice of carrot cake.

When it came to cuisine, he never looked too far beyond the oxtail soup and the box of cheese and the mixed grill. And certainly he never envisaged a day when there'd be men in Ireland who'd be turning up their noses at the mixed grill, at a fine plate of rashers and eggs and sausages and fried bread and tomatoes and mushrooms and black and white pudding and maybe a slice of liver and maybe even a lamb chop, if it was a high class aytin'-house. And tea and bread and butter, of course.

Now he has to listen to various quacks explaining that the mixed grill, and the fry itself, one of the few things that the poor ould fellas enjoyed eating – when they were able to eat – will kill you.

Well, they didn't kill the poor ould fellas, who ate nothing but the fry for the best part of seventy-five years, who somehow stayed alive on that lethal regime for long enough to be watching some quare fella on *The Afternoon Show* getting the horn as he marvels at how far we've come from the days of the mixed grill in an aytin'-house to the days of the dinner party, where they laugh at such things.

They just need to say the words "mixed grill" and they laugh, as they nibble their carrot cake and quaff their fine wines, drinking to the death of Old Ireland, where poor ould fellas are still out there throwing rashers onto the pan and thinking it's food.

Not that they do it with any enthusiasm any more, and many's the time they'll end up giving the rashers to the poor ould dog, Mick, who is better able for it.

The necessity of eating is further complicated today by one of the great irritations of modern life for the poor ould fellas: trying to open the bloody packet, can, bottle or carton in order to reach the food or drink inside. Nevertheless, it is something that must be done, a daily trial which is accompanied by swearing and threats of retribution against the manufacturers until the task is finally completed, perhaps brought to conclusion by a helping hand from an obliging niece, nephew, passing postman or district nurse.

And for the record, since the birth of modern Ireland there has been no instance – not a single one – of a dinner party at which a poor ould fella was present. In fact, the poor ould fellas don't eat "dinner", as such, they eat "the bit of dinner", more commonly pronounced "the biha dinner".

So the poor ould fellas are not exactly in hot demand on the dinner-party circuit, even to provide some freakish amusement between courses with their uncouth ways.

Otherwise they would tell their hosts they have established a clear link between food, especially fine food, and bullshit, on a sliding scale which a means that the larger the amounts of fine food, the purer the bullshit – in fact, they are inextricably linked.

No, they don't want to hear that in the dining rooms of the bourgeoisie.

Yet in this gluttonous age, in many ways the attitude of the poor ould fellas to food is grounded in a philosophy which is far deeper than anything buzzing around the mad head of some arsehole TV chef.

When they think of the great men of their time, the poor ould fellas think of Mahatma Gandhi before they think of Gordon Ramsay. And Gandhi didn't bring down the British

The poor ould fella's "Roll of Honour"

Walter Brennan
Batty Brennan
Walter Huston
Harold Steptoe
Cyril Cusack
Noel Purcell
Jimmy O'Dea
Éamon de Valera
Kirk Douglas
Private Godfrey in *Dad's Army*
The poor ould fella who was married to
Anna Nicole Smith
Shane MacGowan

Empire by thrashing it all out at a delightful dinner party. On the contrary, he made a virtue out of eating nothing at all and liking it.

Then there was de Valera, who may not have had the flamboyance of a Gordon Ramsay but who represented his country on the world stage with some dignity, his ascetic appearance suggesting that food played no part in his life and that it should play no part in anyone else's life either.

Most of all, when the poor ould fellas think of great men, they think not of Gordon Ramsay, or even Gandhi or de Valera if it comes to that. They think of the man who is without question the greatest of them all, a man by the name of Lester Piggott.

Over the years, riding all those Derby winners, Lester made money for the poor ould fellas, which is rare enough in itself. But that's not why they revere him.

For a start, they revere him because he did all that without eating any food worthy of the name, maybe an occasional stick of celery just to keep himself alive, but certainly there'd be nothing for Lester on the dinner-party circuit.

The food wouldn't interest him, of course, but the fine conversation would have no attraction either for him. He was almost deaf, so the poor ould fellas can relate to that. But even if Lester had perfect hearing, the poor ould fellas reckon that you wouldn't find him anyway at a dinner party, or any other occasion involving food, wine and friends, holding forth on the issues of the day. Or, to put it another way, bull-shitting.

Because Lester is one of the few men who ever lived who had no bullshit in him at all. He hardly said anything, to anyone, about anything, and when he did – maybe a few astute remarks to Vincent O'Brien after riding another Derby winner – whatever he said was totally lacking in bullshit.

He couldn't hear most of the bullshit that was going on around him, and when he did he pretended not to. And when he couldn't pretend any more, he would mumble to himself and to anyone who could understand him, asking for the bullshit to stop so he could get on with his work in a bullshit-free environment.

And when the respectable classes cheered at Lester's demise, when they celebrated his conviction for tax evasion, if anything the poor ould fellas revered him even more. They did not join in the laughter about Lester on his first day in prison, meeting this big bald beefy bloke in his cell. "Ah, Mr Piggott, it's a pleasure to meet you," the beefy bloke says. "I've never ridden a Derby winner before."

And while it came as a shock to many, to the poor ould fellas it came as no surprise that a man of Lester's stature, who had led a life that was blameless except for a few accounting issues and a fondness for the smokes, a man who did his job without complaint, though he was often hungry and thirsty, a man who was famously free of bullshit, should be rewarded at the end, not by the highest honours his country can bestow, but by three years in jail.

That just about summed it all up for the poor ould fellas, who haven't quite been rounded up and incarcerated themselves on some similarly flimsy pretext, but who feel that it's only a matter of time. Till then, they will be treated more or less like criminals, without the inalienable rights which are accorded to criminals as they leave the court laughing and joking, having been miraculously acquitted of 4,857 charges of burglary, assault and battery of poor ould fellas in every county in Ireland.

So when Lester went to jail, the poor ould fellas were even tempted to write to him, the way that those mad women write to the fellows on Death Row. But that would just be more bullshit.

Suffice to say that they identify and empathise strongly with him, as indeed they identify with the poor ould fella who ate the money, which is where we came in.

This true story concerns a poor ould fella who lived with his ungrateful daughter on a farm in one of the border counties. And when one day she told him she was engaged to be married, this pleased the poor ould fella, as he assumed she'd be moving out and leaving him alone.

Alas, when she told him the name of the man she intended to marry, the poor ould fella was aghast. It was the son of an old enemy of his of the other persuasion. So to register his protest, he simply refused to eat the biha dinner she put in front of him each evening. Instead, in silence, he would go upstairs and take out a biscuit tin in which he kept his life savings – he could never actually spend any of this money; he was constitutionally incapable of it. He could only save it, hence the term life savings rather than life spendings.

He would open the biscuit tin and take out various bank-notes of large denominations and bring them downstairs.

And then, still without uttering a word, he would proceed to eat the money.

He would simply put the banknotes into his mouth and eat them, while the daughter watched her inheritance going down his gullet with a mixture of horror and awe.

And this went on for weeks, the poor ould fella refusing to give in and the daughter likewise refusing to budge in her marriage plans – she was stubborn like her father.

And when the poor ould fella died, after the last of many illnesses brought about by malnutrition and general neglect, they counted the money that was left in the biscuit tin, and they estimated that he had eaten approximately £14,000.

But he had made his point.

Hollywood Greats they like

Spencer Tracy
Sophia Loren
Ingrid Bergman
John Wayne
James Stewart
Brenda Fricker

Lament for the Honda 50

It is almost spooky the way that poor ould fellas end up on the wrong side of almost every public issue in Ireland today. You'd nearly suspect that there's a vast conspiracy against them, except in order to conspire against someone, you'd need to give a damn about them one way or the other. You'd need to recognise their existence in the first place.

So when some county councillor straight from central casting laments the drink-driving laws and how country folk can no longer have the few pints and drive home without worrying, no one points out that it's the poor ould fellas who have perhaps suffered most in this area, through no fault of their own.

After all, poor ould fellas are most unlikely to be driving home insanely from the pub in souped-up sports cars, ripped to the tits on crack cocaine, playing games of "chicken" with other poor ould fellas. It would be against their nature.

They are unlikely to be driving home at all, because there's no point in them driving there in the first place, due to the smoking ban.

And if they did make the effort and struggle down to the local bar in the poor ould jalopy, the roads they'd be using would be so remote and so neglected they'd be unlikely to encounter another soul, in any condition.

But in the not-too-distant past, the poor ould fella riding a Honda 50 used to be a familiar sight in rural Ireland. The Honda 50 was a great ould yoke for the bad roads, and it gave the poor ould fellas a bit of freedom, which they used sparingly – often you would see a poor ould fella sitting on a Honda 50 rigid with fear, or perhaps with porter, or some combination of both, riding home at about eight miles an hour.

It didn't go much faster than the ould black bike, but it was a natural progression for the poor ould fellas to switch from the black bike to the Honda 50 when the aches and pains in their poor ould bones didn't allow them to get up on the bike any more.

And in its modest way, the Honda 50 seemed to work for them, and for everyone else, after a Fair Day during which the poor ould fellas might consume several pints of porter and even a few whiskeys.

We recall a poor ould fella in Killorglin, County Kerry, who, after a long day drinking quiet pints, would ask for his Honda 50 to be pointed in the general direction of his home, twelve miles away. Often he would bid farewell with the words, "I wish that the River Laune was flowing with Guinness and that my mouth was big enough to swallow it all."

Somehow, though such men mightn't be entirely sober, you'd never hear of them on Honda 50s causing motorway madness. You'd never hear of them racing other poor ould fellas down the boreen for a bet. Somehow, the Honda 50 did the job and no more, and at times it seemed to go by itself, if its owner was perhaps a bit shook.

It was cheaper than the ould jalopy, it wasn't hard on juice and, being made in Japan, it usually worked. So what happened next?

What happened to these excellent machines which were of such inestimable value to the poor ould fellas?

Obviously, they stopped making them.

Obviously, there would be no point in making something any more just because it greatly improved the quality of life of the poor ould fellas. Like I said, you'd think there was a conspiracy afoot, except somehow you suspect it's something worse than that, a sort of systematic annihilation of all the little things that made their lives vaguely bearable.

And on that Honda 50 they would sometimes need a few hot toddies inside them for two main reasons – to keep out the cold and to steel themselves against what they might find when they got home.

"Intruders", perhaps, or if they're lucky, nothing but Mick the dog. Nothing which might soften the message which is coming to them with total clarity: They Are Expendable.

Cars they like

something that will just get me around ...

Ford Anglia
Morris Minor
Volkswagen
The postman's van

Cars they don't like

BMW, Porsche, Alfa Romeo, Ferrari,
Lexus, Mercedes
Jaguar, Range Rover
The stolen sports car
containing drug-addled
inner-city youths
which screeches up the
lane in the dead of night

Songs they like

"The Irish Rover" – Pogues with The Dubliners
"Wooden Heart" – Elvis Presley
"Little Arrows" – The Dixies
"I Was Born under a Wandrin' Star" – Lee Marvin
"The Streak" – Ray Stevens
"Sloop John B" – The Beach Boys
"(I Hear the Sound of) Distant Drums" – Jim Reeves

Songs they don't like

"Escape (The Pina Colada Song)" – Rupert Holmes
"Firestarter" – The Prodigy
"Sisters Are Doing It for Themselves" – Aretha Franklin and Annie Lennox
"Bermuda Triangle" – Barry Manilow
"Summer of '69" – Bryan Adams
Anything by Celine Dion or Oasis and everything else recorded during the last thirty years

DISEASE,
DYSFUNCTION
AND DEATH

The Ailments

By definition, the poor ould fellas have been around for a long time. They have somehow stayed alive for at least six decades, though they might have wished it otherwise. So you'd imagine that the gurus would be coming over here to compile a best-selling book about the lifestyle of this strange tribe, analysing the reasons for their longevity, observing them in a scientific way and taking copious notes.

You'd imagine that the gurus would be studying the dietary habits of the poor ould fellas over a long period of time and, on a broader level, trying to discern their overall philosophy.

You'd imagine that, but you'd be wrong.

Because for the gurus the poor ould fellas are an unsettling phenomenon. For a start, they do not approach each new morning with a rush of positive energy and optimism and enthusiasm. In fact, they approach it with an entirely negative attitude. They don't want to seize the day: they want to kill the day.

And this is not exactly the sort of uplifting message we tend to hear on the talk shows from the authors of uplifting books.

Dylan Thomas famously wrote about his poor ould fella raging against the dying of the light, but mostly the poor ould fellas rage against the coming of the light through the curtains every morning, signalling another difficult and meaningless day to be endured somehow.

And from the moment that another day starts, they are willing it to end, ideally slipping away in a fitful sleep at about seven in the evening and eventually waking up far too early – not that they particularly want to wake up at any time.

In Ireland today there's a lot of bullishness, a lot of people "going for it", trying to live each day as if it's their last. Meanwhile, the poor ould fellas are living each day hoping it will be their last.

So whatever got them through seventy years and more on this earth, it wasn't the power of positive thinking. And on an even more discouraging note for anyone wanting to have a runaway American best-seller based on the ancient wisdom of poor ould fellas, they have stayed alive mainly on a diet of cigarettes with an astronomically high tar content, and porter and whiskey, and the most basic of processed foods.

Not only has this regime kept them alive, it has kept them thin. All over the world, there are women going slowly insane trying all sorts of weird diets and philosophies, and here we have the poor ould fellas without a pick on them, with a body-shape that most of these unfortunate women are desperately trying to attain – and the message is to smoke unfiltered fags and to drink porter and whiskey and to eat processed cheese and oxtail soup and to live each day hoping it will be your last.

And there's one more thing. It is called hardship.

The poor ould fellas, as they say, "got hardship".

It would be virtually impossible to replicate the sort of hardship which the poor ould fellas got growing up in Ireland long ago, but suffice it to say, it would not be a very attractive proposition in a modern Western context. Most of the abuses which the poor ould fellas suffered as a matter of routine are now illegal and carry lengthy prison sentences for the perpetators – savage beatings, for example, at home and at primary school, for no reason; psychological and sexual abuse by priests and religious; hunger and cold and hopelessness and brutality of all kinds – yes, the poor ould fellas got hardship.

But they're still here. They're still alive.

Not necessarily alive and well, just alive. But that itself should be an inspiration to all of us who are constantly being told that smoking and drinking and eating rubbish and being depressed all the time will kill you.

Sadly, even for the most intransigent poor ould fella, there comes a time when a trip to the doctor just can't be put off

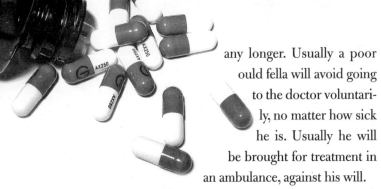

any longer. Usually a poor ould fella will avoid going to the doctor voluntarily, no matter how sick he is. Usually he will be brought for treatment in an ambulance, against his will.

He hates the cure far more than he hates the sickness. He hates being examined by the medics; he hates their soft hands poking him. He even hates the fact that they're trying to make him better, when on balance he would prefer to get worse, very quickly, so he could go away and die.

For the poor ould fella, a chronic heart condition can be seen not as a problem, but as an opportunity – not in the New Age sense, but in the sense that death may be near, and thus he won't have to exist any longer in a world which also contains *The Afternoon Show*.

The ailments which afflict the poor ould fella tend to be chronic by the time he presents himself to the medical profession. He is not the sort of man who will have a routine check-up every six months, so whatever is wrong with him tends to fester away for years or even decades before he is hauled in front of the men in the white coats.

Or even the women in the white coats. As if the world of medicine wasn't already fraught with peril for the poor ould fella, he now has something new to fear: this deep dread that he'll be brought to an appointment thinking the doctor is a man, only to find that it's a woman, casually telling him to take off his trousers.

Weather Forecasters they like

Michael Gilligan

Weather Forecasters they don't like

None (except Martin King)

More bad weather ...

"Just take off your trousers there," he hears the woman's voice saying again and again in this nightmarish vision, "just take off your trousers there," as if it was the most normal thing in the world.

Anyway, he doesn't need any of these characters to tell him what's causing the old lumbago. He knows that it can broadly be attributed to a liftetime of lifting things. Heavy things, that he probably shouldn't have been lifting at all. Things that no one lifts any more, because there's probably a law against it. And there might even have been a law against it when the poor ould fella was doing all the heavy lifting, but of course no one bothered to tell him about it.

So he doesn't feel that these doctors who have never in

Newsreaders they like

Charles Mitchell
Don Cockburn
Maurice O'Doherty
Andy O'Mahony
Eileen Dunne

More
bad news ...

Newsreaders they don't like

None

their lives lifted anything heavier than a fountain pen to sign a big fat bill for services rendered have much wisdom to impart on these matters. And his reluctance is understandable, because he knows from looking at other poor ould fellas that once they fall into the clutches of the Irish health service they are bollocksed. Completely and utterly bollocksed.

From the moment they are diagnosed, by a "caring professional", their quality of life, such as it is, deteriorates horribly. It's not the pills that they mind so much, it's the journeys to the Mater Hospital in Dublin to receive some horrendous treatment every month for whatever ails them.

Invariably, they are sucked into these dreaded routines, to get a blast of radiation or a shot from a syringe or to have the dressing changed on a wound after a recent amputation.

This can go on for months or even years.

The journey to Dublin can be made even more excruciating when they are brought to Guineys or Clerys to buy a pair of pyjamas or even a dressing gown, a terrible trial for these men.

Little wonder that if they have a touch of the old lumbago they have this awful fear of going to the doctor, in case they end up on the monthly shuttle to the Mater to receive treatment for about forty other major life-threatening illnesses that the medic has discovered from one urine sample.

And they'll still have the lumbago, only now they're on steroids and chemotherapy and all sorts of terrible shit that is supposed to make them better … and for what?

Frankly, the poor ould fellas themselves can't derive much joy from the best-case scenario held out to them, being ferried up and down to the Mater so that junior doctors who are a bit nervous with the needle can get some target-practice, so that they can make their greenhorn mistakes on patients who are technically alive but who don't really count – the undead.

Here the poor ould fellas from rural parts have just one small advantage over their less isolated brethren.

For them there is a more agreeable best-case scenario, based on a certain piece of equipment which they have at home and which allows them to administer a treatment to themselves, one with an extremely high success rate.

A wintry smile plays upon their lips as they contemplate it, waiting for them at the end of another long ride from the Mater.

It is called a double-barrelled shotgun.

And it is loaded.

Films they like

You can't call them 'indians' any more ...

Doctor Zhivago
The Bridge over the River Kwai
Gone with the Wind
The Sound of Music
Oklahoma!

Special Category – Cowboy Pictures:

She Wore a Yellow Ribbon
Gunfight at the OK Corral (not the modern remake)
Cat Ballou
Butch Cassidy and the Sundance Kid

Films they don't like (by the sound of them)

Brokeback Mountain
9½ Weeks
The Magdalene Sisters
Lock, Stock and Two Smoking Barrels
Love, Actually

The Area of Sexuality

For the poor ould fellas, there is no such thing as sexuality. Or not in any meaningful sense, anyway.

The word "sexuality" has never been uttered by any poor ould fella, at any time, or in any place, in any context of any kind.

It is another bullshit word which was never heard before 1974 or thereabouts, a notion dreamed up by people with very little to bother them and too much time on their hands.

The word "sex" itself doesn't arise in the lives of the poor ould fellas for any reason except when they might be filling in some Department of Agriculture form about livestock. Otherwise they would no more give a name to the act of procreation than they would give a name to one of their cattle, which, like sex, is just something that comes and goes and is probably more trouble than it's worth.

Sex, for the poor ould fellas, is something that happens, mostly to other people – it's not something you talk about. Certainly some poor ould fellas have been married, and some of those have even had sex. Not great sex, not good sex, but not bad sex either. Just sex. Or what we generally call sex, we who need to name these things and discuss them over dinner like Miranda and Carrie in *Sex and the City*, debating the merits of the so-called golden shower.

Certainly a poor ould fella would get the horn from time

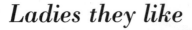

Ladies they like

Sophia Loren
Grace Kelly
Maureen O'Hara

Ladies they don't like

Sinead O'Connor

to time, but that's life. He wouldn't get it from watching Internet porn, because he doesn't know that the Internet is, and if he does, he doesn't admit it. Nor does he get it from making immoral and illegal approaches to his four-legged friends, as popular myth would have it – poor ould fellas actually have very little interest in bestiality because, apart from anything else, we just don't have the weather for it.

And even if they were inclined to be chasing a goat around the field, looking for the ride, they wouldn't have the legs for it.

They would get the horn from reading the *Sunday World*, but it would go away soon, or they would make it go away, and then they could settle down for an afternoon enjoying one of life's few genuine pleasures, listening to the sport on the radio.

Since almost all of them were violently sexually abused as children, by a wide variety of authority figures, they rightly regard sexuality as an extremely dark area, not a suitable subject for merry banter after a few glasses of Chardonnay at the book club, when talk naturally turns to the pros and cons of taking it up the arse.

Favourite Friend

Courtney Cox

she's very fresh looking …

That would not be for them: they hate all that bullshit, though they don't feel especially bitter about their own "sexuality" being stunted by the abusive climate which prevailed in old Ireland – since it happened to almost everyone, you'd nearly think there was something wrong with you if you had somehow been left out.

Sometimes, after watching Sophia Loren on an old Hollywood movie shown on morning-time TV, they would get a bit nostalgic for the days of their youth, when after a few bottles of porter they would imagine themselves squiring the lovely lady through the streets of Rome, with Sophia doing all the talking and them just nodding and smiling, wearing a hat and a nice suit.

122

That, too, would give them the horn.

But even in this romantic vision they could never see themselves buying flowers for the lady, because they have a mental block about that sort of thing, probably the result of Catholic teaching which reserved floral tributes for statues of Our Lady, not the lady you might be taking to dinner – which is another black spot for the poor ould fellas, who could never conceive of a situation in which "the biha dinner" would be a prelude to anything except back-breaking labour.

Not for them "the biha dinner" with the lovely lady followed by a romp in the Jacuzzi.

They don't understand any of that ould carry-on, but Sophia Loren is still a lady they like, a real lady of the type that no longer exists. In this era of Sinéad O'Connor, there's very little out there for the poor ould fellas when it comes to ladies.

Of the current crop, they have a great liking for Eileen Dunne who reads the news on RTÉ and who has the genetic advantage of being the daughter of a GAA commentator. They'd have a great liking for her, even a secret passion, but they would never talk about it.

Yet in their own quiet way, the poor ould fellas can give voice to this deeply rooted thing called sexuality, such as it is.

It's just that they don't do it in the manner prescribed by the experts, all those men who sound like failed priests, lisping away on RTÉ about their frigging sexuality.

To give an example of the poor-ould-fella way around these things, it is worth relating a true story about a scene which unfolded in a public house on the outskirts of Drogheda, County Louth, some time in the early 1980s.

The bar was quite busy and many of the customers were poor ould fellas, enjoying a drink and a smoke in the afternoon before shuffling away to let the younger clientele enjoy the evening untroubled by the serene wisdom of poor ould fellas.

And there was a certain novelty to the proceedings, as the proprieter had just installed a video machine, videos being a relatively new-fangled arrival in rural County Louth. On this day, he had decided to show the critically acclaimed and surprisingly popular film *Quest for Fire*.

Directed by the Frenchman Jean-Jacques Annaud, with a "script" by Anthony Burgess, it told, as the title suggests, the story of primitive man's efforts to make his life more manageable, his earliest attempts to relate to his surroundings, to conquer his fear and his ignorance and to search for a source of fire.

Of course, they did not speak in any recognisable language but in a primitive tongue specially created by Anthony Burgess.

And of course, they were all naked most of the time, because they had no clothes and they knew no better.

And as the film developed in its strangely poignant way, primitive man was also seen engaging with the mystery of primitive woman.

From the most brutish beginnings, eventually they would share the odd moment of tenderness.

The poor ould fellas watched all this in silence, supping their pints and puffing their fags. Then there was a climactic scene featuring primitive women on the bank of the river, washing in the water, bending over as they worked. Lust-maddened, a number of primitive men approached the primitive women from behind and humped them in the most perfunctory manner as they went about their task. Having done the deed, the men ran away grunting and shrieking.

As they digested this piece of action in the bar on the outskirts of Drogheda, there was a certain discomfort in the body language of some of the poor ould fellas.

An uneasy silence descended upon the gathering.

And then one of the poor ould fellas cleared his throat to speak. He spoke perhaps the most eloquent words ever uttered by any man on this difficult subject.

"There was snow today in Ardee."

Dogs they like

Mick

Dogs they don't like

Pekinese
Poodles
Dachshunds
Chihuahuas
Various greyhounds

That'll be another trip to the vet ...

No Hugging,
No Learning

The makers of the classic comedy series *Seinfeld* had a rule – there would be no hugging and no learning. You see this rule quoted often when people are discussing the genius of that programme, its hold on the popular consciousness in the 1990s and beyond.

There would be no heart-warming scenes of characters ending a dispute with a big old hug, each realising that the other might have a point after all and promising to learn from the experience.

No hugging and no learning. There was too much of it about, too much that was trite and touchy-feely, too much moralising. And the makers of *Seinfeld* are to be congratulated for sticking to this, for refusing to succumb to the temptations of hugging and learning, as *Frasier* did with such lamentable results.

So well done, Jerry, and well done, Larry David and all the gang. Except it should be pointed out that they weren't quite the first people in the history of the human race to espouse this philosophy. They weren't the only ones who held the line on this against all odds.

They were only doing in a fictional setting what the poor ould fellas have been doing in real life for as long as anyone can remember and with no end remotely in sight.

So if *Seinfeld* is to be applauded for its integrity in this regard, how much more laudable is the iron resolve of the poor ould fellas in the no-hugging and no-learning stakes? For the poor ould fellas, there is no reward, no eight million dollars an episode. For them, it's not even a conscious decision, it's just a gut reaction, an instinctive refusal to play the game.

And to the poor ould fellas that's all it is – a game. There's no substance to it, no real meaning to all this hugging and

Tough guys they like

James Cagney
Edward G. Robinson
Humphrey Bogart
George Raft

Tough guys they don't like

Arnold Schwarzenegger
Sylvester Stallone
Everyone in *EastEnders*

learning. In fact, there was no hugging at all in Ireland until quite recently, and then suddenly it took off like a new dance craze.

Somehow Ireland had survived centuries of hardship without any hugging, and then some time around the mid-1970s or thereabouts it all changed. Maybe it was the result of too much exposure to English and American television; maybe the Irish just lost their way – who knows the exact point at which a society starts getting it all wrong?

Perhaps it started off just as a form of social climbing. The gentry were always thought to be quite keen on hugging, at least behind the high walls of their estates. But the majority of the people were made of sterner stuff, and some of them still are.

Anyway, from its modest beginnings back in the 1970s, hugging has now reached epidemic proportions in Ireland. Women hug men they've never met before, men hug women and, most depressingly for the poor ould fellas, men hug other men. Even if no drink has been taken, they can be seen embracing when there is no need for it at all, when a handshake would suffice.

But on the whole, women are the worst offenders. On the very rare occasions when a woman is introduced to a poor ould fella, she will offer her cheek demurely to the poor blighter, expecting a little peck or something.

The poor ould fella doesn't know what she wants, exactly, all he knows is that he's not able to give it to her. At least, not the way she wants it.

There's a sort of a knack involved that the poor ould fella

doesn't have, because he wasn't raised that way.

He comes from a place where people had boundaries, where they weren't throwing themselves at one another in this fashion.

In modern parlance, they gave each other space. They kept a critical distance. In fact, they gave each other a whole lot of space, to the extent that hugging and pecking and all this close bodily contact was almost unknown among happily married couples, let alone among people who had barely been introduced to one another.

It wasn't expected and it wasn't done, especially in situations where it might make people uncomfortable – and that meant almost all situations.

But then this way of being in the world, with all its decorum and its admirable retraint, started to go out of fashion, even in Ireland. If you held on to the old ways, you might find yourself being condemned as a "repressed" individual. And there was apparently nothing worse than being repressed. It was considered most unhealthy to be repressed. For a person to be healthy, they needed to be tactile, they needed to be making public displays of affection, at all times.

And they would think nothing of inflicting these displays of affection on men who didn't welcome it at all. Actually, the poor ould fellas could justifiably regard this as yet another form of bullying and abuse, this pressure that is constantly being put on the poor ould fellas to join in with all this excess of emotion, this falseness.

There's nowhere for them to run, nowhere to hide. In any social setting, they're in a state of constant dread, knowing that at any moment someone they hardly know will offer them the cheek to be pecked or wrap them in a fond embrace for no reason at all, leaving the poor ould fellas mortified, just praying for it to be over and hoping against hope that they won't accidentally headbutt their tormentor in the clinches.

They know too that the perfumed women are pretending not to be horrified by the strange odours that waft from the suits of poor ould fellas, who feel that dry-cleaning is not for them.

So the body language of the poor ould fellas is not the best in these circumstances, and again, this is seen as unhealthy by the sort of people who fail to ask themselves this question: if the attitude of the poor ould fellas is unhealthy, why then do the supposedly healthy people who have put all this repression and Catholic guilt behind them spend half their lives babbling away in the psychiatrist's chair?

If they are so emotionally well adjusted, why don't they feel the pain of the poor ould fellas when they're subjected to these appalling rituals, these ordeals of kissing and hugging and unwanted molestation in general?

And as for the process of learning – the so-called wisdom which comes with the resolution of some emotional problem – why can't they see how the poor ould fellas are suffering in these situations and learn not to do it again?

"Learning" is not for the poor ould fellas either, and that is their prerogative.

They know enough.

Sportsmen they like

Christy Ring
Mick Mackey
Ronnie Delaney
Cassius Clay
Lester Piggott
Kieron Fallon

Sportsmen they don't like

Cristiano Ronaldo
David Beckham
George Foreman

He's always looking for penalties ...

Because They're Not Worth It

In the psychobabble of today, the poor ould fellas have issues around self-esteem.

You will not find them anointing their bodies with the oils of the Orient, making themselves fragrant. You will not find them spending much time in the Body Shop sniffing the soaps.

Indeed it would be rare enough to find a poor ould fella in the shower at all, because they still regard the shower as a relatively new-fangled thing, especially in parts of rural Ireland where there are plumbing issues.

So when the poor ould fellas wake up and try somehow to summon up the courage to face another day, it rarely occurs to them that a power shower may be just the thing they need to liven them up, not to mention a dollop of shampoo and a hint of shower gel by l'Occitane en Provence.

No, they don't see themselves leaping out of the shower to continue their ablutions with a shave, using the Gillette Mach 4 battery-operated razor, with a fine lather created by Nivea for Men and perhaps even a sinfully indulgent splash of shaving balm, again from the Nivea for Men range.

Indeed, they hear these ads for the Nivea for Men range while they're listening to the bit of football on a Saturday afternoon, and the ads merely provide further proof that the whole of the male species is in danger of extinction, with the poor ould fellas the first to go, followed inevitably by the younger men who have been demoralised to such an extent they have effectively turned into women, with their gels and their balms and their sprays and their perfumes "pour homme".

All this is killing them softly, while the poor ould fellas are going down hard.

So it is rare for the poor ould fellas to pamper themselves in this way, or in any other way either. Between the poor ould fellas and the *pour homme*, there is a vast chasm.

They see these quare ones on the ads for l'Oreal, finishing with the line "because you're worth it", and they are bemused. Because no one ever talks to the poor ould fellas like that. No one ever tells them they're worth a damn, and in fact no one *has* ever said such a thing to them, in all their days, if truth be told.

The poor ould fellas have come to believe that bad things are always happening to them because they're not worth it. They have issues around self-esteem, for reasons that are both natural and unnatural. It is natural that they have an extremely low opinion of themselves simply as a consequence of growing up in Ireland long ago, when this was the only sort of opinion which was tolerated.

And then there are all the unnatural factors which have occurred along the way and which we are trying to describe in this book, knowing that it would take another twenty-five books just to give a flavour of the myriad forms of abuse to which these men are subjected and the basic human rights which are denied to them. Because they're not worth it.

Moreover, the makers of antiperspirants and deodorants are not targeting their multi-million euro campaigns at the poor ould fellas, who are conspicuous by their absence from commercials for Lynx and Sure and Right Guard.

Clearly, they remain to be convinced that if they use a certain deodorant they will soon be ambling up and down Copacabana beach like bronzed gods, wearing nothing but a posing-pouch and pair of dark glasses, giving the glad eye to the tanned Brazilian lovelies and then dancing the night away to the beat of the samba.

Somehow, no matter how many drugs the poor ould fellas might be on for their various ailments, they can never quite see themselves in that vista.

If they're on certain medication, that vision might give them the horn, but they know it's not for them, and it's probably not even for poor ould fellas who live in Brazil – no doubt they have their own crosses to bear in a society that worships the body beautiful. But as far as we know, unlike their Irish counterparts, they can at least smoke in the bars.

And typically, in neglecting themselves in these areas, the poor ould fellas are also doing the rest of us a favour. They may not be as obsessed as the average teenager with issues of personal hygiene, but they are better in the eyes of God. Because if they were spraying themselves morning noon and night with deodorants, as younger men are encouraged to do, they would be causing further damage to the hole in the ozone layer. But since they take no part in this dangerous bullshit, they are doing their bit for the environment.

And getting no thanks for it, of course. When TV's Duncan Stewart is touring the countryside, marvelling at the solar panels which have been installed by some smashing young couple and praising them for their progressive approach to the environment, he rarely, if ever, stops at the door of a poor ould fella to show his appreciation for what that man is doing for all of us by refusing to use aerosols of any description.

The poor ould fellas will not use an aerosol for reasons of personal vanity, nor will they use one to make the air more fragrant, and they certainly won't use one to kill flies, because the way it is, when there are a few flies in the house maybe the poor ould fellas don't feel so alone. In fact, they appreciate the company.

Nor will you find the poor ould fellas luxuriating in a hot bubble bath, sipping Chardonnay and listening to a heart-rending love song by Christopher Cross and crying. That's not their style.

There are men in Ireland today who have a Jacuzzi in their own home, but none of them are poor ould fellas. The Jacuzzi is a totally alien concept to the poor ould fellas, who are deeply suspicious of bathing in all its forms, as they were raised in an atmosphere of shame and mortification of the body.

Toothpaste itself holds even fewer attractions for the poor ould fellas. You will not find them sitting around the fire debating long into the night the merits of the Colgate ring of confidence as against the minty fresh Macleans or the ultra-white Ultrabrite. For men who have lived through a world war and a civil war and many other wars, public and private, this would not be a burning issue.

They have seen all the ads, and still they feel that plaque and "sensitive teeth" and "acid erosion" are among the least of their problems. As for "flossing", they don't even know what it is.

And they are unlikely to find out, since they only have a few stumps left and they simply refuse to go to a dentist. Under any circumstances.

The poor ould fellas can be bullied into just about anything except a visit to the dentist, unless they can be guaranteed that if the tooth-puller puts them to sleep in the chair they'll never wake up. And while there are many in officialdom who would welcome this development in back-door euthanasia for poor ould fellas everywhere, it is still technically illegal – another example of the law failing to keep up with the mood of the times.

Soap itself is not to be found on every poor ould fella's sink, though they would usually pack a bar of Imperial Leather in a plastic bag if they were forced into the Mater Hospital for the operation. As for everyday use, they wouldn't be too bothered, they wouldn't be too fussy, but they find it handy to use a bit of soap instead of shaving foam when they're scraping away at the poor ould whiskers with a Bic disposable single-blade razor, which they've been using with diminishing success since 1998 or thereabouts.

The poor ould fella figures he's outwitting the ad-men here, with their spray-cans of green shaving goo. He's saving himself a few bob and it gives him a certain glow of satisfaction, which darkens almost immediately when he cuts himself, as he invariably does, the blood mingling with the soap and pouring down his poor ould withered neck.

At this moment, the fact that he is also saving the ozone layer is scant consolation.

Strangely, the poor ould fellas are not entirely free from the tyranny of the multinational toiletries industry, as they will perhaps have a bottle of Old Spice on the sink, which was given to them by the nephew back in the 1970s.

They think they might use it in an emergency, say if they found out that they were going to be examined by a lady doctor. And even though the bottle has been tightly sealed for approximately thirty years – no more than an ornament, really – they fear that it might have gone sour. And how would they tell the difference anyway between good Old Spice and bad Old Spice?

Sometimes they wonder if the bottle is so old it might fetch a tidy sum at Sotheby's. Maybe it's an antique now, worth thirty grand, and they'll never know for sure, but they'll always wonder …

Such are the fears which haunt the poor ould fellas as they try to make themselves comfortable on the cold porcelain of an outside toilet, with a force-ten gale threatening to blow the door off the hinges.

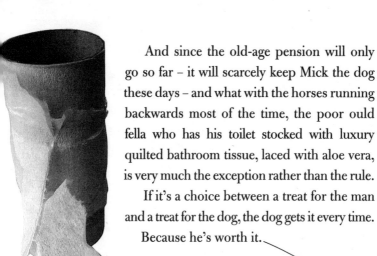

And since the old-age pension will only go so far – it will scarcely keep Mick the dog these days – and what with the horses running backwards most of the time, the poor ould fella who has his toilet stocked with luxury quilted bathroom tissue, laced with aloe vera, is very much the exception rather than the rule.

If it's a choice between a treat for the man and a treat for the dog, the dog gets it every time.

Because he's worth it.

Organisations they like

The Irish Nurses Organisation

They say it's nearly all Nigerians ...

Organisations they don't like

An Taisce
ASH (anti-smoking organisation)

That ban was the worst thing that was ever done in this country ...

The Black Women

When they read about the plight of asylum seekers, the majority of Irish people with their comfortable lives feel quite detached from it. They have this vague sense of some nightmarish bureaucracy, of queues outside the Department of Justice and a form of internment which is taking place in what used to be Butlins.

While they hope it doesn't get too ugly, it doesn't really concern them.

But it concerns one particular section of the native Irish, on a number of levels and in a quite complex manner.

When the poor ould fellas first saw the asylum seekers, and immigrants in general, they felt estranged from them. The poor ould fellas who had lived and worked in England had slaved alongside the black people and knew their ways. But it was still a most peculiar thing to see them arriving in large numbers in Ireland itself. And as for the poor ould fellas who had never been off the island, the sight of Africans and Asians strolling around places like Rooskey and Ballaghaderreen was simply bizarre.

Until this startling new development, a poor ould fella could have spent his whole life in Ireland without ever encountering a person of a different colour in real life. Genuinely, he could go from cradle to grave dealing only with the white man. And while he wasn't extra happy with

141

this state of affairs, he wasn't unhappy about it either. It was just another of those things over which he had no control, just as the arrival of all these coloured folk was something over which he had no control – no matter what happens, it is something over which the poor ould fella has no control.

Indeed, he feels in general that life is something that is mostly arranged while he's out of the room.

But as the realities of asylum-seeking and immigration began to take shape, the poor ould fellas realised that perhaps they had something in common with these dark strangers. Perhaps, indeed, they had more in common with them than with the pasty-faced bureaucrats who were arranging their lives for them and making a complete bollocks of it all.

Yes, this rang a bell with the poor ould fellas, the idea that some arsehole, with the stroke of a pen, can destroy your life. And you can't even go to the pub any more and have a smoke to console yourself.

These feelings of empathy increase when the poor ould fellas contemplate the lot of the asylum seekers banged up in Butlins for the crime of having nowhere to go except this place called Ireland. Suddenly the poor ould fellas start wondering if by any chance the pen-pushers have something similar in mind for Irishmen of a certain age and a certain disposition?

After all, if the poor ould fellas were all rounded up and put in a camp, the authorities could "look after them". They wouldn't have to be bothering the gardaí, who have better things to be doing than finding the sixty-five-day-old corpses of poor ould fellas decomposing in their remote dwellings.

But the poor ould fellas have a race memory of places where harmless poor devils were put so that the authorities could "look after them". They were called asylums and they were feared and hated.

So the poor ould fellas would tend to be asylum avoiders rather than asylum seekers. But they understand that the unfortunate black men who are pleased to call themselves asylum seekers would probably call themselves anything you liked if it meant not having to go back to whatever shithole they came from.

Like the poor ould fellas, they would settle for very little. Indeed this is perhaps the most maddening aspect of it: the fact that your poor ould fella and your asylum seeker are asking for such small things and are being shunned in ways that suggest they are asking for a million dollars in used banknotes and a stretch limousine to the airport and a private plane out of the country just to start the negotiations.

But it's not just this feeling of solidarity that connects the poor ould fellas to the New Irish. Certainly the poor ould fellas wouldn't like to see people being shipped back to Africa for no good reason, but there is more than just principle at stake here.

The fact is that the poor ould fellas have developed a liking for the black women.

You can sometimes see a few poor ould fellas sitting on the bridge below the town, having a smoke, transfixed by the sight of some African woman walking by, perhaps in traditional costume. It is not just the woman herself who captivates them but what she symbolises, a strange and wonderful world beyond these shores of which the poor ould fellas can but dream.

They recall their lost youth, when the traditional costume of Irishwomen, by contrast, was a more modest affair, somewhat less colourful, designed as much to repel as to encourage the attentions of the predatory male.

And, of course, with their black suits the poor ould fellas themselves could be said to have a traditional costume of sorts, even more modest in style.

Now, so late in life, they can view this daily parade of beautiful black women. It is at once a source of quiet pleasure and a source of sadness for the ships that passed in the night.

Newspapers / Magazines they like

Sunday World
Ireland's Own
Racing Post
Farmers Journal

Newspapers / Magazines they don't like

The Irish Times
VIP

The Road to Nowhere

As they struggle on towards the end of their days, the poor ould fellas come under certain pressures from the caring professions. They are encouraged to go to day-care centres and the like, to go on coach trips, and to indulge in group activities which are supposedly good for them.

Though their old bones are oh-so-weary, they are encouraged to get out of the house and get themselves involved in these activities and make friends with other poor ould fellas who are coming under similar pressure from bright-eyed and apparently well-meaning young people, who only have their interests at heart.

Or have they?

In whose interest is it, exactly, that the poor ould fellas are kept on the move in this way? In whose interest is it, exactly, that the poor ould fellas are taken to places where they can be observed at all times by trained professionals?

Clearly the main purpose of these exercises is to try to ensure that if a poor ould fella drops dead, at least someone will notice that he has dropped dead and appropriate measures can be taken. Not only must the poor ould fella die, he must be seen to die.

Always in the mind's eye of a member of the caring professions is that scarifying image of the poor ould fella found dead in his hovel weeks, or months, or even years after

146

he has dropped dead, or been bludgeoned to death, or some unhappy combination of both.

A very ugly scene there for all parties. But for the poor ould fella lying dead, the aftermath is not so terrible, because he is, after all, dead.

He's gone to a better place. And even if he's gone to no place at all, it's still a better place than the place he was in.

No, for once, the poor ould fella is feeling no pain, walking through the valley of the shadow of death with a certain pep

Alcoholics they like

George Best
Shane MacGowan
Errol Flynn

He could really knock them back …

Alcoholics they don't like

The ones that write books about it and are interviewed on *The Afternoon Show*

in his step, while the men in the white coats and the surgical gloves and the masks do the necessary.

So for the poor ould fellas the benefits of all these supposedly life-affirming activities are negligible. In fact, it is mostly a pain in the arse to be herded round in this manner,

for all the world like children at the nursery-school stage.

Indeed, Shakespeare suggested that in the seventh age of man there are strong echoes of childhood, and it seems that various state agencies are determined to make the seventh age of the poor ould fellas so childlike they will eventually be wheeled home in prams by their day-care provider, sucking on dodies. Whether they like it or not.

Certainly the authorities feel entitled to treat poor ould fellas as children in the sense that they're expected to do exactly what they're told and to realise that others know what's best for them. And to realise, moreover, that just because they might enjoy doing something, it doesn't mean they're going to be allowed do it.

Thus the poor ould fellas are expected to go on these balls-achingly boring coach tours, which would only be vaguely bearable if they were allowed to smoke on the bus. Which of course they're not.

Obviously they have no desire to see the Ring of Kerry, because in this life, frankly, they have seen enough. And while a seemingly endless bus journey to Kerry might kill the day, on the whole the poor ould fellas would prefer to kill the day by sitting in that busted old armchair by the fireplace smoking fags, looking at a John Hinde postcard of Connemara on the wall, a charming view of Ireland which was sent to them back in 1973 by a nephew who hasn't been in touch since.

Instead they're thrown together in this high-handed fashion and encouraged to participate in sing-songs, again almost exactly like children in a nursery school. Except children aren't usually required to join in renditions of "A Bunch of Thyme" by Foster & Allen or to listen appreciatively as some crazy old crone with a piano-accordion does a horrible, twisted version of "The Boys of the County Armagh".

These treats are reserved uniquely for the poor ould fellas, further weakening their will to live. And all so that various nurses and doctors and minders of every description can be close to them when they conk out for the last time. All so that the professionals can be relieved of the burden of finding the poor ould fellas stretched out in their own homes.

And then there's all the anxiety that the poor ould fellas suffer when they're out of the house without the poor ould dog, Mick.

Naturally Mick isn't allowed to go with them to the day-care centre, or on the bus to the Ring of Kerry, perhaps because that might make the poor ould fellas happy – again, like the child, they might want it, but it wouldn't be right.

It would make the lives of others just a bit more difficult, so that's the end of that.

But the poor ould fellas worry about Mick when they're bullied into leaving the house without him. They're looking at the Ring of Kerry but they're thinking about Mick.

As they imagine all the bad things that might be happening to Mick, their only true friend, they die many times. They die, but somehow they are still alive, the undead who envy the dead, spared that old witch singing "The Boys of the County Armagh".

All they want to do now is go home.

Drinks they like

Stout
Whiskey
Bass

Drinks they don't like

Ballygowan "Still" Water
Low-alcohol Guinness
Extra Cold Guinness

ENTERTAINMENT
AND LEISURE

Puppetry of the Penis

As a rule, the poor ould fellas wouldn't be "into" the theatre.

They would have no opinion on the controversial reloca-
tion of the Abbey Theatre or other bullshit subjects such as
the direction in which the Abbey is going, artistically.

As far as the poor ould fellas are concerned, since the time
of Lady Gregory the Abbey was never going anywhere even
remotely close to where they live, artistically or any other way.

And now that you can't even have a smoke there, for the
poor ould fellas the Abbey assumes a level of irrelevance which
the human mind can scarcely quantify.

Not that they haven't seen the odd good play in a lifetime
of theatre-avoidance. *Big Maggie* by John B. Keane wasn't
bad, and there was another one by John B. Keane that wasn't
bad either ... or so they heard, anyway.

But it was a long time ago. And John B. is dead now.

Nor did this one good experience whet the appetites of
the poor ould fellas for those magical nights of theatre at the
Gate, with Louis Le Brocquy and Anne Madden in the audience watching Friel's adaptation of *Uncle Vanya* or Ralph
Fiennes "giving" his *Faith Healer*.

Though they lack a grounding in critical theory, somehow
the poor ould fellas have always had this amazing intuition
about the theatre, this gift for taking the most basic information
abut a play – sometimes they wouldn't even need to know

the title, they'd just need to know it was a play – and knowing in an instant that it was complete and utter bullshit.

If only the theatre-going public had a fraction of the nous of the poor ould fellas in this regard, they could have saved themselves an awful lot of pain over the years.

But they don't. So they can be found with their arses going numb, trying to pretend that they find Beckett funny, because they read about how funny he was in *The Irish Times*.

Now the question of whether Beckett is funny may be vaguely interesting. But it's not nearly as interesting as the fact that his plays are full of what can only be described as poor ould fellas.

They look like poor ould fellas, and they wear black suits like poor ould fellas, and they are deprived of almost all hope or comfort in this life like poor ould fellas.

Beckett, it could be said, based the bulk of his oeuvre on the poor ould fellas and the way they are in the world, but you wouldn't hear this mentioned at the famous Beckett Festival, which was launched at a lavish reception attended almost exclusively by rich and glamorous people getting a great ould kick out of watching poor ould fellas scratching around in dustbins and waiting to die.

So while the poor ould fellas are in the theatre, at least in the plays of Samuel Beckett, they are not *of* the theatre.

They are alienated from all aspects of the theatre, the artistic and the social, the mainstream and the radical. Especially the radical.

So you would not find them foaming at the mouth in anticipation of the Dublin Fringe Festival, or looking back nostalgically at nights long ago in the Project Arts Centre, watching Nigel Rolfe rolling around naked on a bed of flour.

All of that stuff kind of passed them by, as they were otherwise engaged with the pick and the shovel, building this place called Ireland, a place where generations as yet unborn can enjoy the work of radical theatre groups such as Puppetry of the Penis.

Yes, the poor ould fellas must have felt it was worth all the hard graft, all the dog's abuse, all the slave wages, when they saw in the paper the following announcement: Puppetry of the Penis – Extra Shows Added Due to Popular Demand.

Now isn't that just grand?

These men can remember the excitement and the pageantry of the Eucharistic Congress, when Count John McCormack sang "Panis Angelicus" and the whole world seemed to stop and listen, just for a while, to the voice of Ireland.

Now they are still alive to see similar levels of enthusiasm for the work of men who put a fellow on a stage with a string tied around his mickey. And at the end of the string there's a heavy object.

Can he somehow lift the heavy object with his mickey? This is the burning question, and the Irish will now pay top dollar to discover the answer, in numbers large enough to have extra shows added "due to popular demand".

From "Panis Angelicus" to Puppetry of the Penis, it's been a long, strange trip. From Panis to Penis, are we sure, are we absolutely sure that we are going in the right direction?

I hasten to add that the poor ould fellas didn't find out about Puppetry of the Penis from reading the arts pages of *The Irish Times* – it was more a case of them seeing a picture of the fellow with the string tied to his mickey in a page of the *Sunday World*, with the mickey blacked out.

And while some of them saw it in the normal course of reading the *Sunday World*, others saw it while perusing the paper which they had torn carefully into strips and placed in the outside toilet in case of emergency – and for the poor ould fellas, of course, any call of nature is something of an emergency.

Imagine then, if you will, the state of mind of the poor ould fella, as he hunkers down in the outside toilet on a wild and wintry night, hoping against hope that that this daily ordeal will reach a satisfactory conclusion, that it will all be over soon, his eyes landing on the picture of the man with the elastic mickey.

Perhaps, at best, it will trigger some memories of a happier time, when the poor ould fellas could relate in some infinitesimally small way to what was happening in the theatre in Ireland long ago.

Perhaps it will bring back images of men like Jack Cruise and Jimmy O'Dea and Noel Purcell, men who could sing and dance and tell a joke without needing to take off their trousers and show their mickeys to the people on the stage of the Theatre Royal.

Those men were artistes who would never have done such a thing, and do you know why? Because it would be too easy.

We recall a poor ould fella telling us about the time he met Mr Noel Purcell himself on a train.

And eventually, when they had exhausted all other subjects, they got talking about the theatre, and Purcell said he could do "blue" jokes, no problem, But he refused point blank to do "blue" jokes. And do you know why he didn't do "blue" jokes?

Because he wouldn't lower himself to that level, he said. Because he was better than that.

That's why.

He was better than that. He was an artiste who did not need to descend to the level of the animals to entertain a crowd.

The poor ould fella got quite emotional recalling these words of Mr Purcell's with tears in his eyes.

It was a meeting with a remarkable man, whereas, in the theatre of today, the most you can hope for is to meet a man with a remarkable mickey.

Northerners they like

George Best

The things he could do with a ball …

Northerners they don't like

Major Ronald Bunting	Mary McAleese
Bill Craig	Johnny Adair
Brian Faulkner	James Galway
Gerry Adams	Dominic McGlinchey
Martin McGuinness	Seamus Mallon
Harry West	Bernadette Devlin
Seamus Heaney	Nigel Dodds
John Hume	Sir John Alderdice
"Doctor" Ian Paisley	Gusty Spence
Ian Paisley Jnr	Ken McGinnis
Dessie O'Hare	Billy Bingham
Billy Wright	"Tucker" Little
David Trimble	Jeffrey Donaldson
Lenny Murphy	Gerry Fitt
Brian Kennedy	George Seawright
John Taylor	Gregory Campbell
Peter Robinson	Mitchell McLoughlin
Phil Coulter	Eamonn Holmes
Austin Currie	Gloria Hunniford
"Rev." William McCrea	Joe Cahill
"Rev." William McGrath	Julian Simmonds

Hoping Against Hope

Despite all that they are forced to endure, by a world that doesn't care, the poor ould fellas still manage to demonstrate the boundless capacity of the human spirit.

They do this when they buy a Lottery scratch card.

Why do they bother? Why don't they just walk away from the shop counter with the week's provisions, the drop of milk and the loaf of bread and the rashers and the sausages and the box of cheese and the packet of soup and the few cigarettes, maybe the small bar of Cadbury's chocolate for that special occasion?

Why do they pause, and weigh up the situation, and decide that buying a Lottery scratch card might be the smart play?

We can't rightly say what goes on in the hearts and minds of the poor ould fellas at this moment, except to suppose that there is something buried deep within all of us, some indefinable substance which allows us to hope for a better life, even when we know full well that all hope is gone.

Maybe they're just feeling a bit flush after collecting the pension. So they hand over their few coins, which constitutes a relatively large percentage of their income and which means that they will probably eat even less well than usual as the week drags on.

They take the card and they start scratching, either in the

161

shop or just outside it where they can prolong the experience by lighting up a cigarette.

In fact, due to the draconian legislation which has outlawed smoking in betting offices as well as in pubs and shops and any other premises in which a poor ould fella might find

himself, this is probably the only way that the poor ould fellas can smoke and gamble at the same time – another hint there, at their possible motivation.

And, of course, they do the scratching either in the shop or just outside it, because if they win an instant prize of €10, they need to be in a position to collect it immediately. Frankly, the odds on a poor ould fella winning an instant prize are roughly the same as the odds on him surviving the week. So this isn't an activity that he can do at leisure, taking his scratch card home in pristine condition and looking at it for a few days, building up for the big moment when he pulls out the penny and starts scratching – and then, if he wins, he still has to get himself back into town to claim the money, hoping against hope that he can get there before he dies.

Anyway, most of the time these matters never arise, as the card is a dud, and the poor ould fella leaves the shop just a bit poorer for his little buzz. But then there's another scenario.

What if he gets three stars, and he signs the card and sends it off, and he's watching *Winning Streak* on the Saturday night and Derek Mooney actually pulls the poor ould fella's card out of the drum?

The prospect that awaits the poor ould fella then is thrilling for a few moments. Yes, as Derek reads out his name, the poor ould fella nearly passes out with the shock. He is elated, seeing himself spinning the wheel and playing all the stupid games and collecting the free money in a huge cheque. And maybe the car … and maybe the holiday in Rio De Janeiro … ah yes, already the vision is darkening, and soon it has assumed all the twisted dimensions of a full-blown nightmare.

Within minutes of getting his big thrill, the poor ould fella is crucified with worry, and soon he is feeling what can only be described as intense fear.

Obviously he hadn't thought it through to this stage when he was making that fateful decision to buy the scratch card. Obviously a poor ould fella could never entertain the notion that he would be spinning the wheel, because nothing as good as that could possibly happen to him, could it?

Well, apparently it could, but not without the hellish

journey into a world of pain which he now contemplates.

He is going to be on television. He is going to be on live television, and the RTÉ types won't let him in the door wearing the suit that he's wearing now, a perfectly good suit which has stood the test of time but which would probably not pass muster with the RTÉ types. So he will have to either get his suit cleaned, which he's never done before because there was no call for it, or else he'll have to submit himself to the appalling indignities of buying a new one.

There will be a journey to RTÉ. He will have to get a taxi and talk to the taxi-driver, two hours of bullshit until he reaches the world headquarters of Bullshit International – RTÉ itself.

Now his blood runs cold at the awful scenes which he anticipates. He will have to meet people, and they too will want to talk to him, probably gay RTÉ fellows will be giving him the paw and coming out with more bullshit and expecting their fair share of bullshit in return. He will probably have to meet women, RTÉ-type women who won't be content to give him the paw, they will try to kiss him, that little peck on the cheek which to the poor ould fella is anathema.

He will have to meet Derek Mooney.

Not Derek Davis, who has a certain bluff geniality and who presented some half-decent afternoon TV shows back in the day. Not that Derek, the other Derek, very much the wrong Derek as far as the poor ould fella is concerned.

He will have to sit there on television while the wrong Derek introduces the poor ould fella to the people of Ireland,

Derek drawing on his own considerable stores of bullshit.

Perhaps the one crumb of comfort is that at least the poor ould fella is totally isolated from the rest of humanity. Which means that he won't have a load of eejits in the audience to "support" him. Unless, of course, a few of the long-lost nephews get to hear about it and arrive at the door looking for a piece of the action, the fuckers.

For all these reasons, and more besides, for many a poor ould fella the prospect of appearing on *Winning Streak* is just too traumatic. So he doesn't appear on the programme at all. His place is taken by some much younger person, a niece or a nephew who "represents" him, playing all the no-brainer games on his behalf, maybe even spinning the big wheel on his behalf, while the poor ould fella sits in the audience, shivering with fear and shame.

He knows that at one level they are doing him a favour, sparing him this ordeal, but on another level they are doing themselves a favour, sparing the nation the unpleasantness of having to look at a poor ould fella on television, raw and uncut.

Now he wonders what got into him at all the day he bought that scratch card.

And he even starts to see *Telly Bingo* in a different light.

Telly Bingo is aimed mainly at poor ould wans, allowing them to indulge their passion for bingo without having to leave the house and get on a bus and go to a hall with a load of other poor ould wans, wasting the time of the driver and wasting petrol and basically wasting space that could easily be filled by much younger people, or people who matter.

But the poor ould fellas find themselves looking at *Telly Bingo* too, because they have nothing else to do.

And because they are intrigued by the presenter, Shirley Temple Bar, who is what is known in the trade as a transvestite. Yes, RTÉ is the only public-service broadcaster in the civilised world that thinks it's a neat idea to have a show for poor ould wans and poor ould fellas presented by a transvestite, a man dressed as a woman. Or is it a woman dressed as a man?

This is what preys on the minds of the poor ould fellas because sometimes, just to take the piss altogether it seems, Shirley appears as a man, wearing men's clothes. But talking like a woman, of course, the woman known as Shirley Temple Bar.

For the poor ould fellas who can remember when TV programmes were presented by decent poor divils like Bunny Carr, this is hard to take. And it's only "lunchtime", as RTÉ calls it.

If they can put a full-blown transvestite in front of the poor ould fellas at "lunchtime", they are capable of anything.

But for certain poor ould fellas, *Telly Bingo* is not all bad. Unlike the Lotto, it doesn't hold out the promise of happiness to the poor ould fella and then take him on this ride to the gates of hell.

When viewed in the light of *Winning Streak*, it is almost humane.

Radio Stations they like

RTÉ Radio 1
Local radio (for sport and deaths)

Radio Stations they don't like

RTÉ 2fm
Raidio na Gaeltachta

The Myth of Daniel O'Donnell

There's a common misconception that Daniel O'Donnell is very popular with old people and those who are old at heart.

This is only half true. He is, of course, loved by old women and women who are old at heart. But he is not loved at all by the poor ould fellas.

Not that anyone notices this, as they lavish attention on all the ould wans who have nothing better to be doing than travelling up to Donegal in buses to kiss Daniel's proverbial ring.

Many, many newspaper articles and radio and TV broadcasts were made about these massive gatherings of ould women, and it apparently occurred to no one to remark that the poor ould fellas were somewhat thin on the ground and that there might be a reason for this.

A very good reason – namely that the poor ould fellas hate Daniel O'Donnell. They hate him, and they hate everything that he represents.

Naturally they hate his music, because it is shite. Which doesn't particularly bother the ould wans, who don't care about that sort of thing, but which reminds the poor ould fellas that good music, of the type played by, say, Johnny McEvoy, has been almost wiped out since the emergence of O'Donnell as a force in the land.

But there are darker and perhaps even sadder reasons for their hatred of him. They know, deep down, that the ould wans love O'Donnell because he's the boy they always wanted their sons to be like – basically, a priestly type who won't involve himself in anything dirty with girls.

While the poor ould fellas tried to raise their sons the right way, by leaving them alone and saying nothing, the ould wans always had this sickly vision in mind. And of course they blamed the poor ould fellas when their sons turned out normal.

The women never really wanted sons who drank pints and backed horses and did all those dirty things. They wanted someone like Daniel O'Donnell. And when he suddenly appeared, towards the end of their days, wearing a white suit and winking demurely at them, they swarmed all over him.

And the poor ould fellas were left to contemplate this disturbing question: if the womenfolk are generally disappointed at the way their sons have turned out, how do they regard the poor ould fellas? If O'Donnell is the perfect being, with his beatific smile and his snow-white suits and his lovely, lovely voice, what are the poor ould fellas, with their downbeat manner and their black suits and their calloused hands?

Something of a work-in-progress, perhaps?

Not that the womenfolk need dwell too long on their disappointments, seeing as how their entertainment needs are so amply supplied by all branches of the industry of human happiness working in harmony. The poor ould fellas could live for a thousand years without ever again seeing a

Places they like

The old Croke Park
The Cliffs of Moher

1950 ... that was the year we went to Rome with Father McKevitt ...

Places they don't like

Dublin

real book, by a real author like Nevil Shute, even in the library – they assume that almost all books are now written by women, for women, so they don't go to bookshops because they're half-afraid they'd be thrown out on account of them not being women.

And they could live for another million years without ever seeing Benny Hill on the telly, Benny who used to give the poor ould fellas a bit of an ould laugh until one day, about twenty years ago, someone discovered that he was grossly offensive to women and also to men of a sensitive disposition.

So that was the end of Benny.

Did it occur to anyone, even for a fraction of a second, that there might be some merit in the comedy of Benny Hill, if only for the fact that it seemed to give poor ould fellas a moment's pleasure, one last miserable chuckle at the end of a long hard road of disease and destitution, one last laugh before they croaked?

Of course it didn't. Because if you got a laugh out of Benny chasing women around with the film speeded up, you were automatically seen as a dirty old man. And that was that.

And what exactly distinguishes a poor ould fella from a dirty old man? Well, a poor ould fella is ignored and quietly despised. Whereas a dirty old man is ignored and loudly despised.

There is a difference.

But frankly, it's not much of a difference.

Not much at all.

And what of all those ould wans drooling over Daniel O'Donnell with their tongues hanging out? Would that not be a bit off colour when the light catches it a certain way?

No, that's fine. It's seen as a marvellous diversion for them, just a bit of harmless fun. It is seen as life-affirming – yes, that's the word, life-affirming.

It is no wonder then that the poor ould fellas regard Daniel O'Donnell, not as a grand man and a most lovely singer, but as a total arsehole.

Shops they like

Guineys (for buying pyjamas before going in for
the operation)
Clerys
Post offices (not situated in a shopping centre)

i'll ask Maureen
to drop into
Guineys to get some
pyjamas ...

"I Will Not Serve in Your Army of Bullshitters"

All of Ireland enjoys a bit of fine weather when we get it. All with the exception of certain elderly gentlemen who stay indoors, unable to enjoy the hot sunshine for all sorts of reasons – physical, spiritual, financial and cultural. Yes, even the weather discriminates against the poor ould fellas.

Let's face it, even if they could afford a bottle of Ambre Solaire to protect their poor ould skin from the effects of the terrible heat, they would not exactly be a welcome sight on the beaches where we worship the body beautiful.

The young people of Ireland would avert their eyes in horror. Sunbathing is simply not an option for a poor ould fella, and he can hardly just sit on the beach in his black suit, because it would just look wrong in these image-obsessed times. And in extreme cases, when the rays of the sun react with the material in the black suit, especially one which hasn't been expensively cleaned for some time, the suit has been known to crack.

What poor ould fella, after all he's been through, would chance a day at the seaside which might expose him to an awful dose of sunstroke, a whole range of social embarrassments and possibly even a big crack in his one good suit?

Signs on it, you will not see many poor ould fellas larking about in the sunshine, though in all likelihood you wouldn't even notice their absence. For most of us, they have simply ceased to exist.

So they stay indoors, out of the heat, excluded once more from life's banquet. They can hardly even be seen at Croke Park any more on the day of a big match, because the new Croke Park is not for them. It frightens them in all sorts of ways, not least because they assume they'll be thrown out for eating their sandwiches and drinking a flask of tea as they traditionally did in the years before the Irish discovered corporate entertainment.

Period of Irish history they'd most like to have lived in

The Past

That must be forty years ago ...

Certainly if there is even a whiff of corporate entertainment in the air – and at the new Croke Park there is considerably more than a whiff – there is no place for the poor ould fellas. Their presence is not required, not appreciated and in many cases openly discouraged.

But once every four years at least, when there's a World Cup about to start, they have something to look forward to, if that isn't putting it too strongly – at least the four weeks of almost constant football will accomplish one good thing. It will kill the day for them.

A lunchtime match, an afternoon match and an evening match should kill at least fourteen days for them, a gift from the baleful gods which they weren't expecting at this late stage.

"Put me down in the chair and layve me there," the poor ould fella will say to the woman from the Vincent de Paul who comes around occasionally with "the biha dinner" and a packet of fags and a few helpful suggestions about how he might improve his quality of life – did he ever think of saving the few shillings he spends backing horses to go to Medjugorje? Or what about going down to the day-care centre to make things out of papier mâché? And would he like to read this great book by Bill Cullen?

And when she comes up with some line about the poor ould fella really needing to get out of the house, he will not engage with this foolishness. He will again refer to the broken-down couch which is pointed in the general direction of the small black-and-white television, and he will say: "Just put me down in the chair and layve me there."

Not that the poor ould fellas are huge fans of the beautiful game, but at least while RTÉ is showing the World Cup they will have something to watch that isn't *The Afternoon Show*. And of course they will have John Giles.

Many people have asked us what is the main source of unhappiness for the poor ould fellas, the one thing above all others which has destroyed what is left of their lives, and we tell them that if you could sum it up in one word, that word would be "bullshit".

All that the poor oul fellas hear, and all that they see, and all that ever happens to them, is bullshit. The smoking ban is bullshit. Betting offices with water coolers and coffee-vending machines are bullshit. *The Afternoon Show* is bull-shit, but then almost everything and everyone who is associated in any way with the media is a purveyor of what can only be described as bullshit.

With one exception.

His name is John Giles.

Almost every time that John Giles has appeared on television for the last twenty years, he has had an open invitation to add in some small way to the world's apparently inexhaustible supply of bullshit. But he has refused that invitation.

He has never stated it explicitly, but it is implied every time: "Yes, I am appearing on RTÉ television in a prominent role, but to Ireland in general, and to RTÉ in particular, I say, I will not serve in your army of bullshitters. I will not serve."

And it is so strange to see a man on television who is not bullshitting in some shape or form, that visitors to this country, who are used to pundits like Ally McCoist and Jamie Redknapp, can hardly believe what they're seeing.

Meanwhile, we Irish have grown accustomed to it over the years, so perhaps we don't properly appreciate the phenomenon. But in their darkened rooms, alone, all alone, the poor ould fellas appreciate it.

In a silent way.

It's Not Good to Talk

We're all talk nowadays. When anything remotely bad happens, anything with a hint of misfortune, we are compelled to talk about it to someone we know, or even to someone we don't know, on a radio phone-in or in the psychiatrist's chair.

The idea of any human activity taking place without some sort of a post-match discussion is an increasingly unpopular one.

You are accused of being repressed and generally backward if you are not prepared to talk about your problems. They say it's good to talk.

But there are certain individuals who would dispute this. The poor ould fellas think that it's not good to talk. In fact, most of the time they think its bad to talk.

As far as they're concerned, talk is mostly something that women do and have always done, and when talk was largely a female activity there was no harm in it.

The women liked talking, and the women were always good at talking, to give them their due.

But now that everyone is supposed to be like a woman, because women are better in every way, talk is required from everyone. In fact, it is not just required: it is demanded.

Because somehow, in this world of women, it is felt that even a poor ould fella might solve his problems if only he could talk about them. If only …

Businessmen they like

J.P. McManus

They say he has a real 'no nonesense' approach ...

If only he could "open up" to someone who would listen to his problems in a non-judgemental way, then the poor ould fella would be in a better place, mentally. If only he could articulate his needs, also in a non-judgemental way, then there might be progress.

But of course, this is bullshit.

As we have explained, the needs of the poor ould fellas are simple and they are modest. In fact there are just two things that they need, and they would articulate these needs quite clearly if anyone could be genuinely bothered to listen to them.

They need to be able to smoke in the pub, and they need

the occasional song performed by Johnny McEvoy on day-time TV.

And that's it, folks.

That all they want, that's all they need, and are we going to give it to them, with all our fine talk?

Not only are we not going to give these things to them, we have taken them away in recent times and many of us have congratulated ourselves on our determination not to give them back.

So we ruin their lives like this and then we say, "Now then, poor ould fellas, what else do you want to talk about?"

Moreover, perhaps there are problems unique to the poor ould fellas which just have no place in the realm of therapy, or any other realm of the conscious or the unconscious.

Take, for example, the case of the poor ould fella who arrived at Dublin Airport one day last summer with a flight booked to Lourdes.

Already he had been through many trials. Obviously he was suffering from a long and debilitating illness which had made the last few years of his life unbearable, so bad that he had actually agreed against all his better instincts to go to Lourdes with a group mainly comprised of poor ould wans flocking around the priest.

Or had he even agreed to it? Maybe he just didn't have the strength to resist when they suggested that the answer might lie, not in the repeal of the smoking ban or the music of Johnny McEvoy, but in the supernatural. Yes, maybe a trip to Lourdes would make it all right.

And when he gave in to them he knew he was facing an ordeal, but he hadn't quite anticipated the full extent of the awfulness which awaited him as he entered the sliding doors of the departure lounge at Dublin Airport.

With the priest leading the way it wasn't too hard to stay with the group, yet the poor ould fella was still afraid of getting lost in the throng. And he was deeply afraid that if he got lost, he might meet Michael O'Leary, chief executive of Ryanair, who would ask him what the fuck he was doing wandering around like this?

He feared O'Leary, because the worst type of bullshitter is the one who says he is not a bullshitter. And that's O'Leary.

Somehow the poor ould fella got to the check-in desk with just one major panic attack. As he searched in the tattered pockets of his suit for his passport, he thought for a moment that he had forgotten to change his few shillings into French money. In his traumatised state, he had momentarily forgotten about the introduction of the euro.

So it was some small relief when he remembered that he didn't have to change his money after all, some small payback for the fact that, in his lifetime, they have changed the money not once, but twice, screwing the poor ould fellas first with decimalisation and then with the euro.

He'd like to "open up" about that to one of these psychiatrists, but they'd just ask him to talk and talk and talk, mainly about himself, as if it was all his fault – to "have a look" at why he was resistant to change. Perhaps because it's bullshit?

And as he was mulling over these matters, he found himself at the top of the queue at the check-in desk. A friendly enough chap did whatever he does with the ticket and passport, looking at the computer screen to check that the poor ould fella wasn't on Interpol's list of the ten most dangerous men in international terrorism, and then he told the poor ould fella to put his battered ould case on the conveyer belt which was running behind him.

So the poor ould fella put the case on the conveyer belt, and then, thinking he was doing the right thing, he put himself on the conveyer belt.

And because it was moving, he sat down.

Staff and passengers alike watched, mesmerised, as the poor ould fella drifted off with the baggage. And just as he was about to disappear through the rubber curtain, they stopped the conveyor belt.

From the looks of astonishment all round, the poor ould fella realised he had disgraced himself. He was overwhelmed with feelings of guilt and shame.

Getting off the conveyor belt, he muttered the words, "I'm from the country."

But that didn't quite explain everything.

And frankly, a thousand hours of therapy wouldn't come close to explaining how such a thing could happen. A hundred thousand head shrinkers would be wasting their time here.

So to boil it down to the essentials, just one more time: let the poor ould fellas have a cigarette with their pint in the pub and put Johnny McEvoy on daytime TV.

Then they'll talk.

Eurovision winners they like

Dana
Clodagh Rodgers
Sean Dunphy (not actual winner but deserved to beat the French lad)

Wednesday
13 December 2006

On Wednesday, 13 December 2006, an extraordinary thing happened.

Mr Johnny McEvoy could be seen singing "The Boston Burglar" on RTÉ afternoon television. Not, we hasten to add, on *The Afternoon Show*, which has turned its back on that type of thing.

It was *Seoige & O'Shea* in the late afternoon that featured a clip of McEvoy singing his classic hit, in the context of an interview with the man himself and his touring partner, Mr Brendan Grace. And it was all too brief, as these things tend to be.

But for all the poor ould fellas out there, whose cause we have championed, it was an epiphany. For some, it was perhaps the last good thing that will happen to them in this life. For many, it was too late.

All through these terrible years of afternoon TV which the poor ould fellas have endured, they have been sustained by this ancient vision of Johnny McEvoy which they knew would probably never come around again. All through this time of Hollywood gossip merchants and flamboyant celebrity chefs and transvestite bingo-callers, they have waited … and waited … and waited … in vain.

Until Wednesday, 13 December 2006, that is, when for a few electrifying moments it seemed that all was right with the world again. "I was born and raised in Boston/A place you all know well/ Brought up by honest parents/ The truth to you I'll tell/ Brought up by honest parents/ And raised most tenderly/ Till I became a sporting blade/ At the age of twenty-three."

It was a clip from an old Phil Coulter show, but even that couldn't take away from the significance of the occasion. Maybe next time Johnny will bring his guitar and he'll let loose there in the studio.

"My character was taken, And I was sent to jail/ My friends and parents did their best/ To get me out on bail/ But the judge he found me guilty and the clerk he wrote it down/ For the breaking of the Union Bank/ You are bound for Charlestown."

The man himself could be seen sitting on the couch alongside Brendan Grace, looking dapper, talking to Seoige and to O'Shea, talking a bit of sense, which is another thing the poor ould fellas don't get much of any more.

A man talking sense, a man not talking through his arse, was there some sort of a TV law passed against this around the time that the black-and-white went and the colour came in?

Whatever, for a short time in Ireland, on Wednesday, 13 December, the bullshit stopped.

And then ... it started all over again.

Favourite Writers

Con Houlihan
Bill Cullen
Eddie Hobbs
Mícheál Ó Muircheartaigh (GAA memories)
Frederick Forsyth
Anyone who writes a good thriller

It must be twenty years since the library closed down ...

Least Favourite Writers
(by the sound of them)

John Banville
James Joyce
Maeve Binchy
Zadie Smith
Bret Easton Ellis
Cecelia Ahern

WHAT THE FUTURE HOLDS FOR THE HOLDS FOR THE POOR OULD FELLAS